The Book of Beach Image

Stress Relieving Designs for Adults &

Kids Relaxation

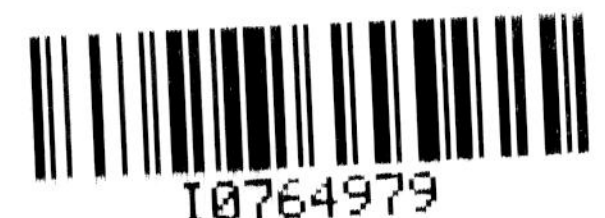

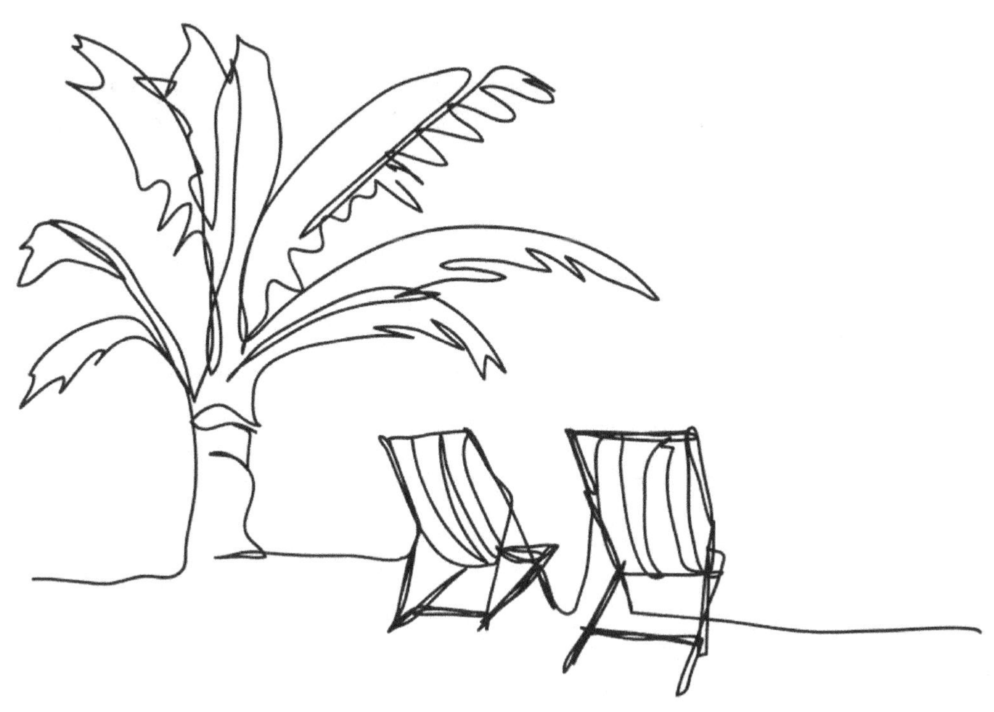

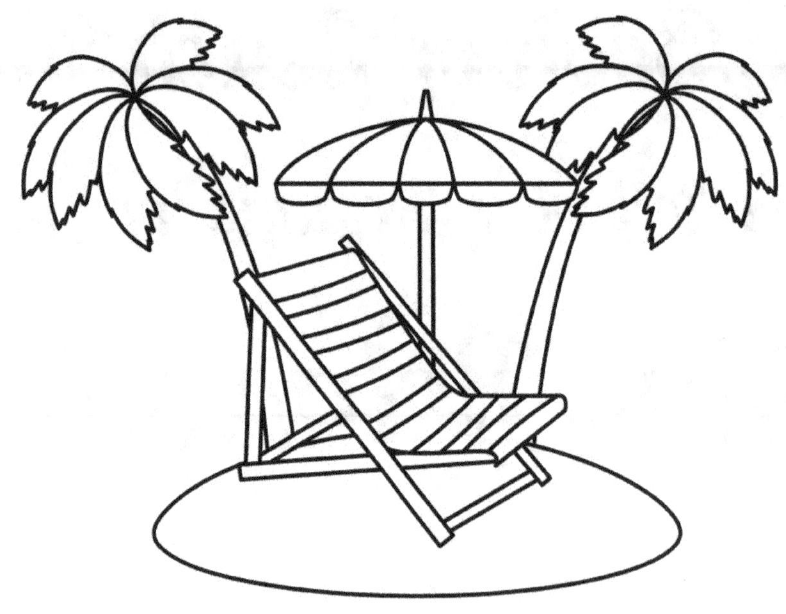

This coloring books is belong to

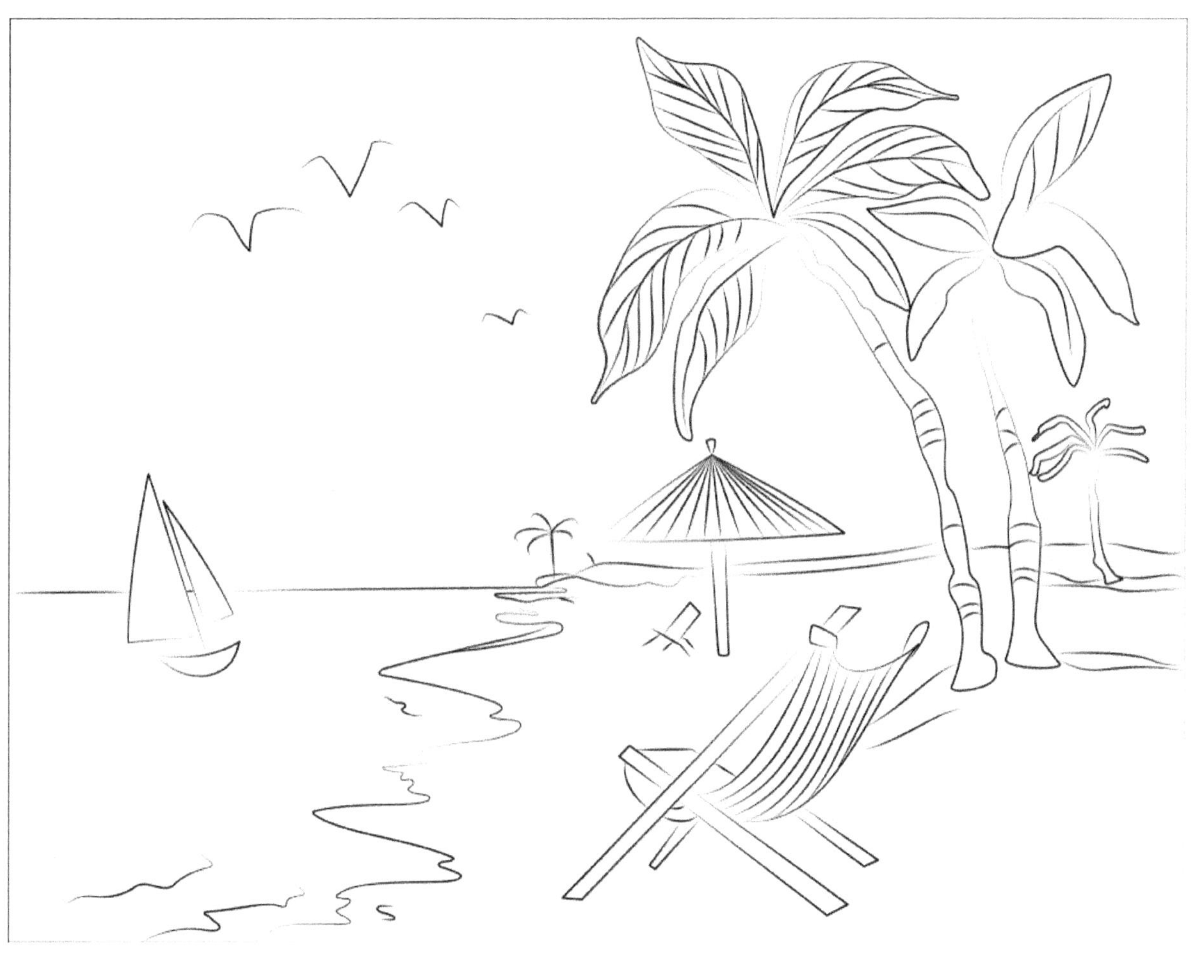

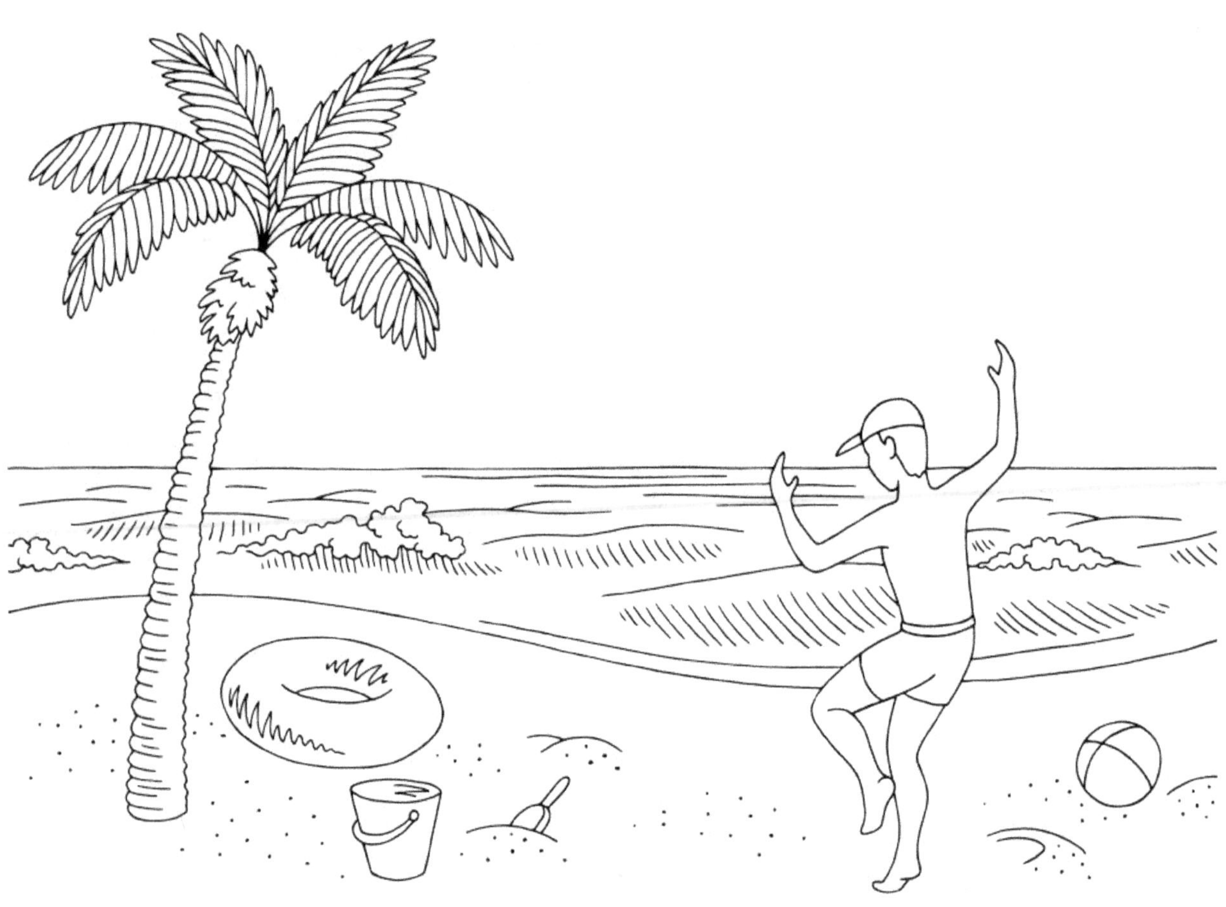

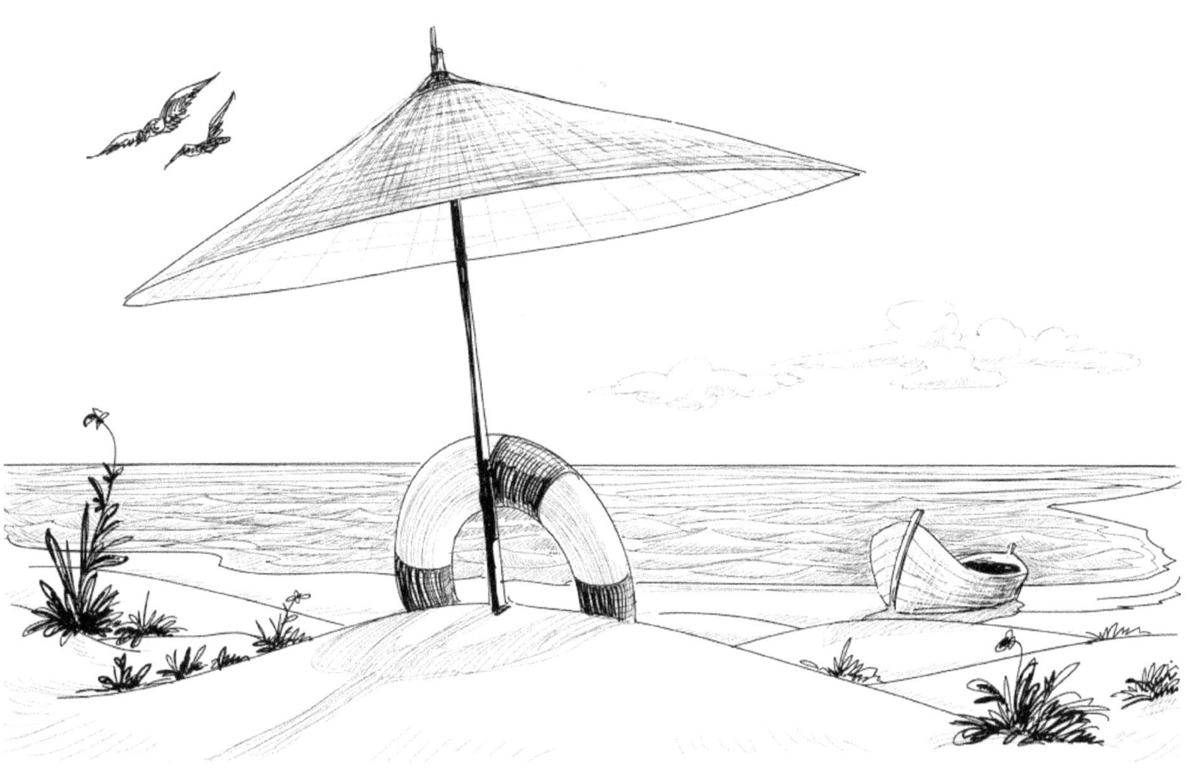

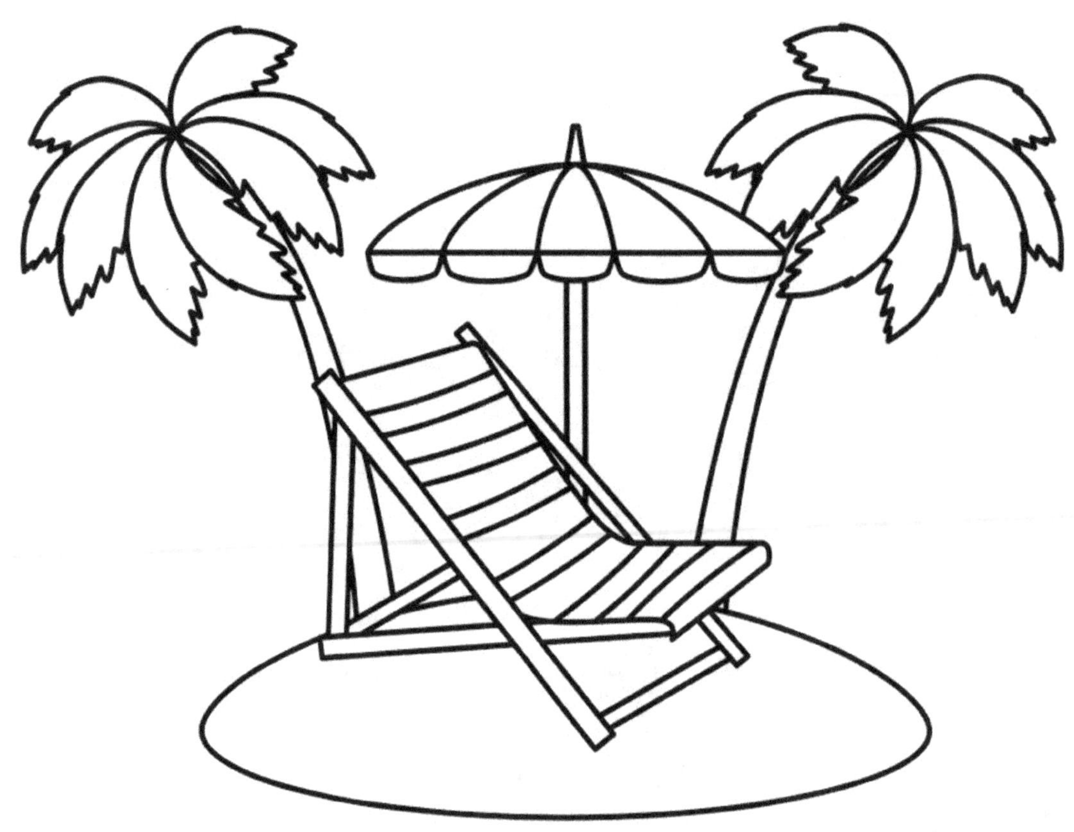

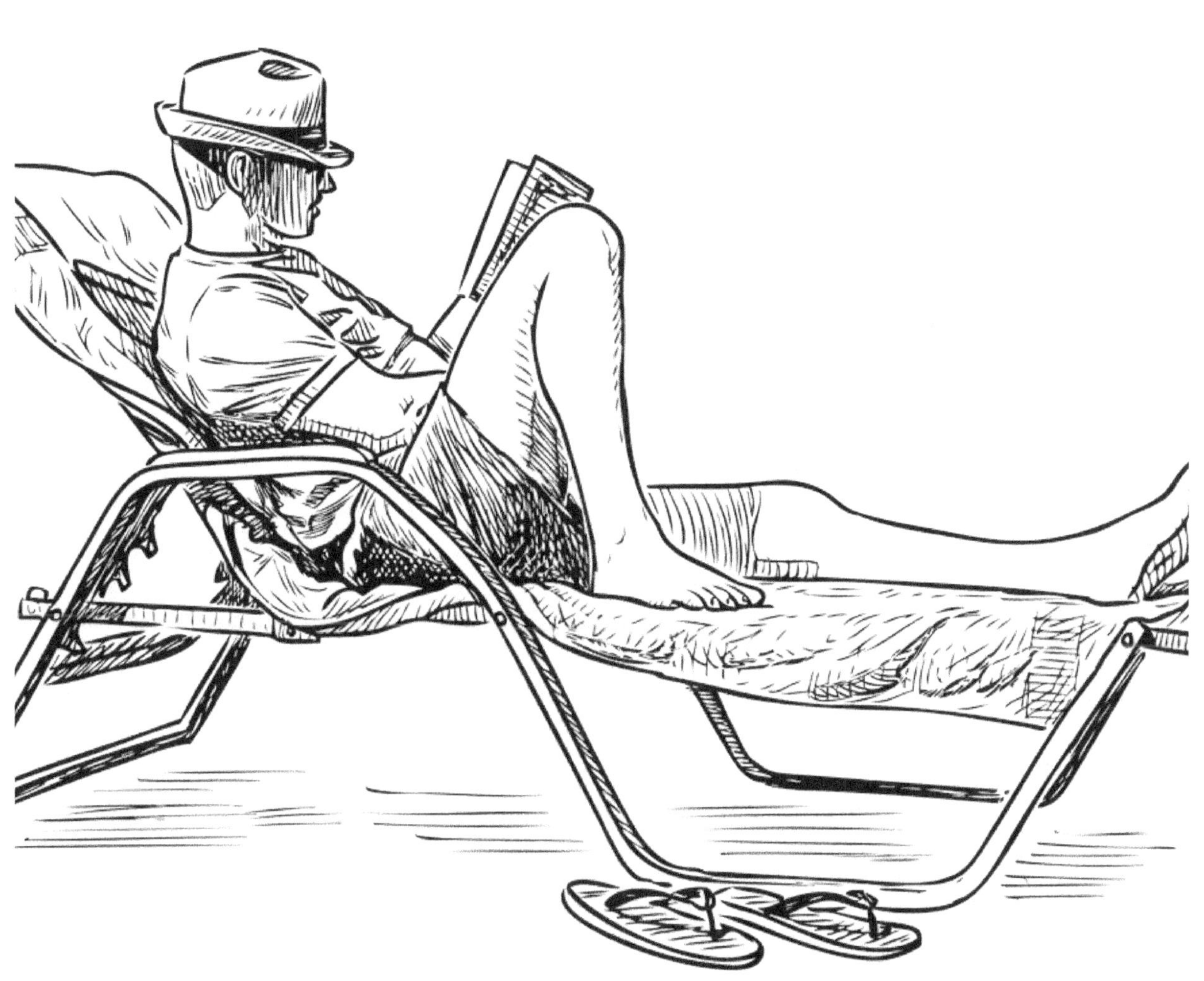

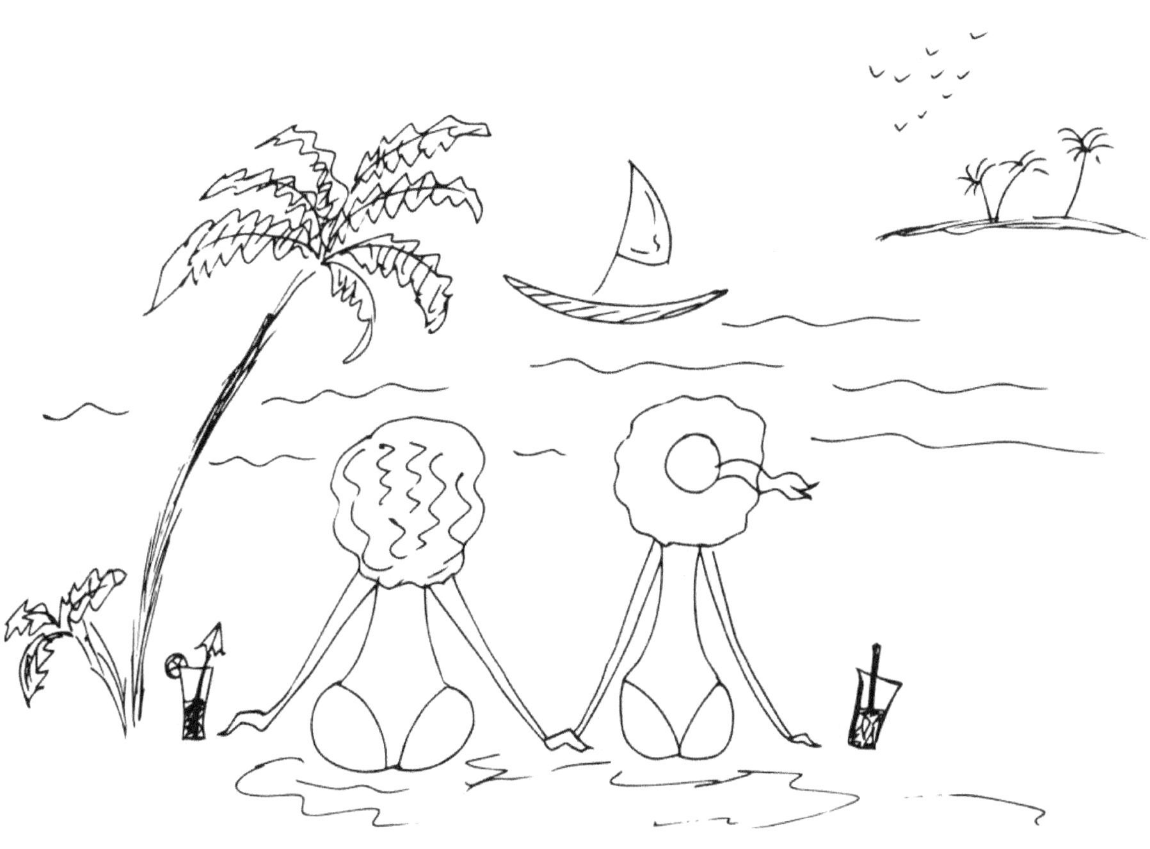

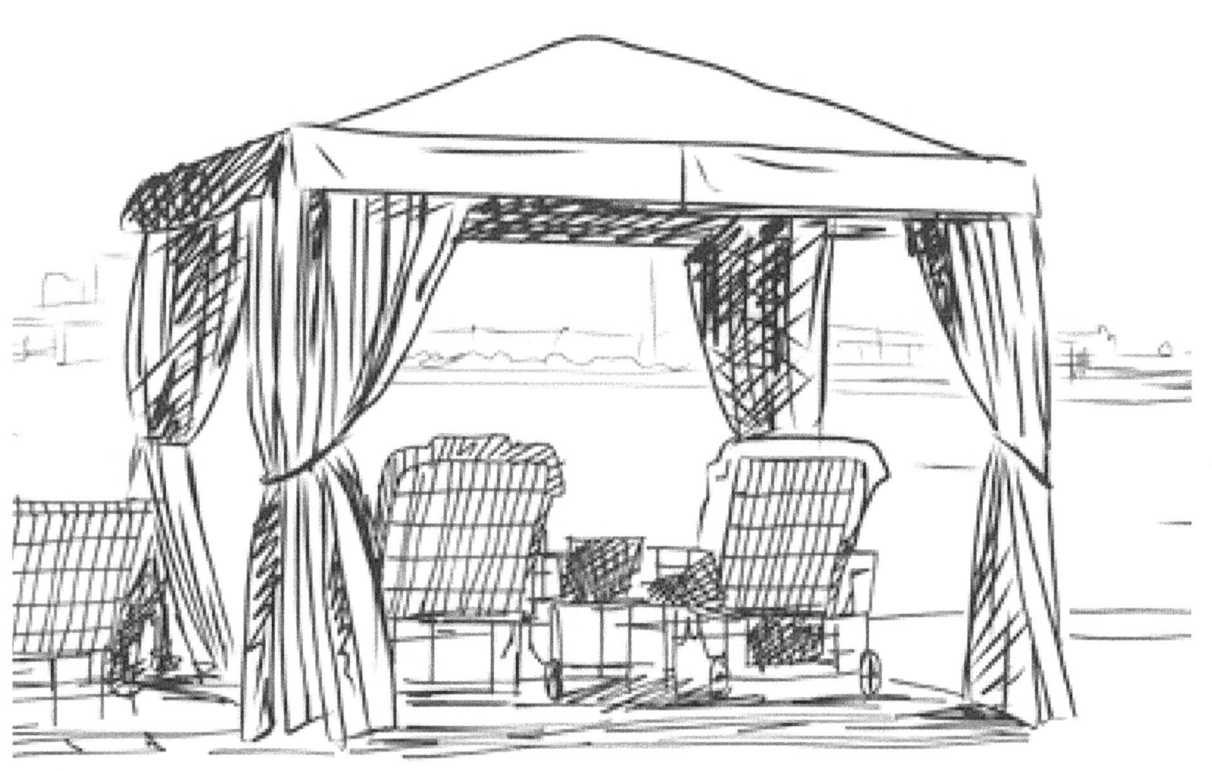

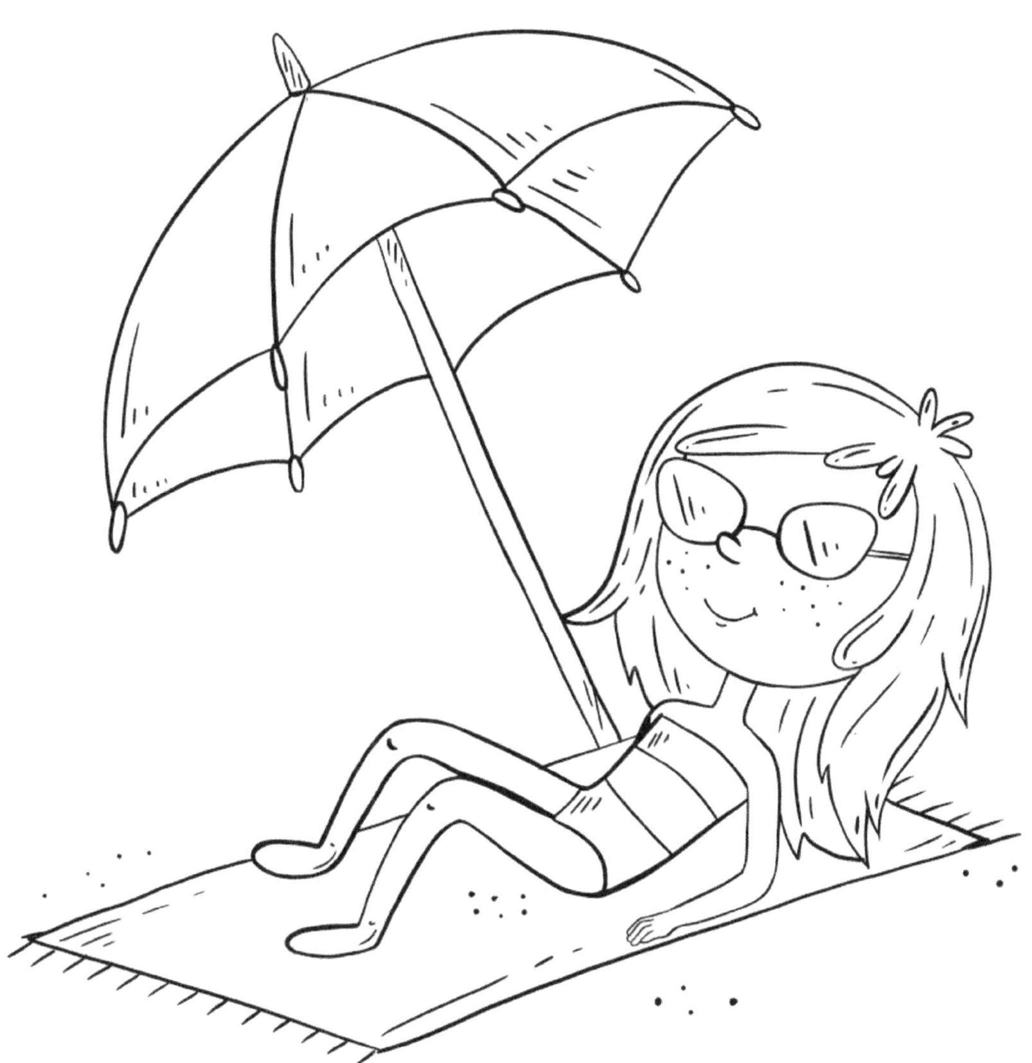

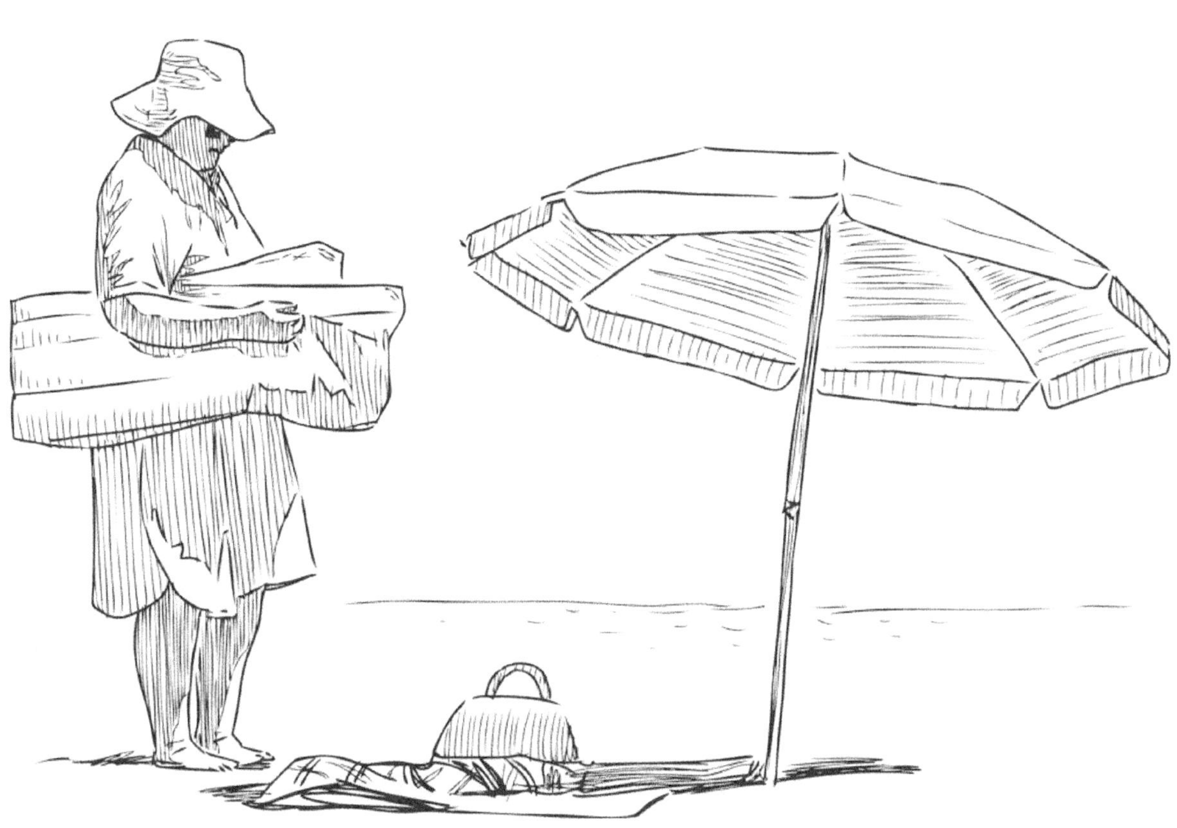

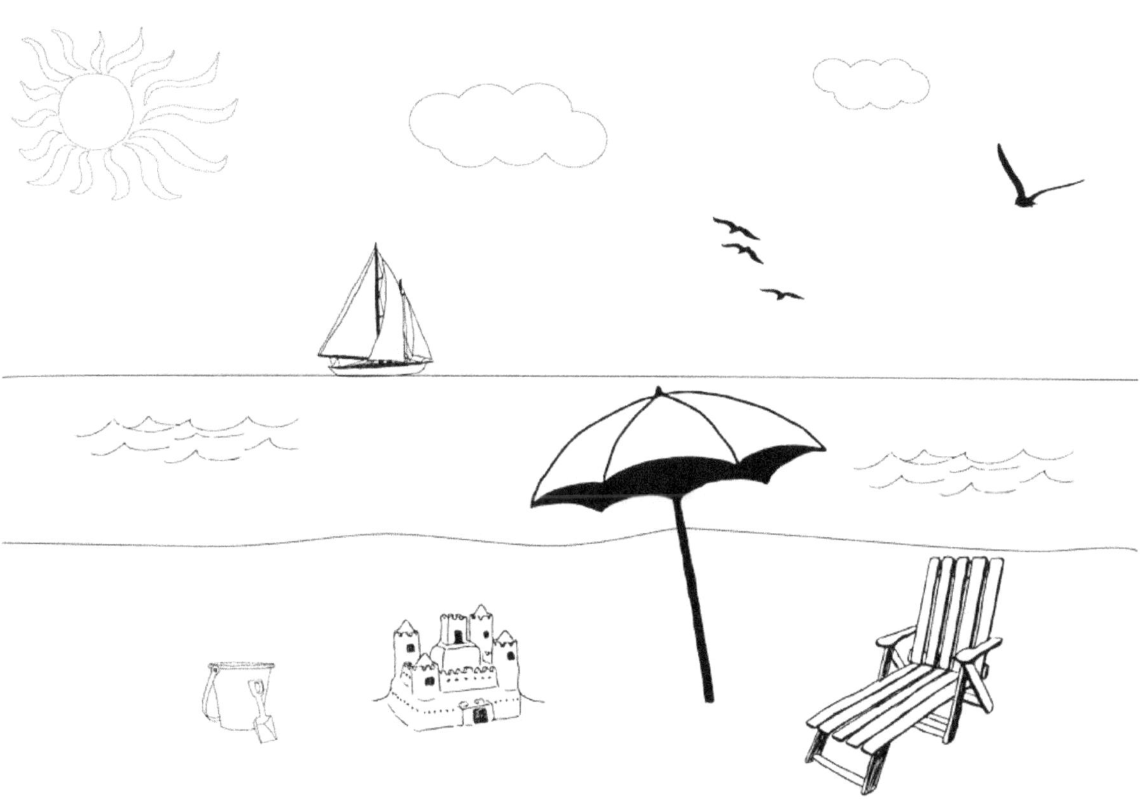

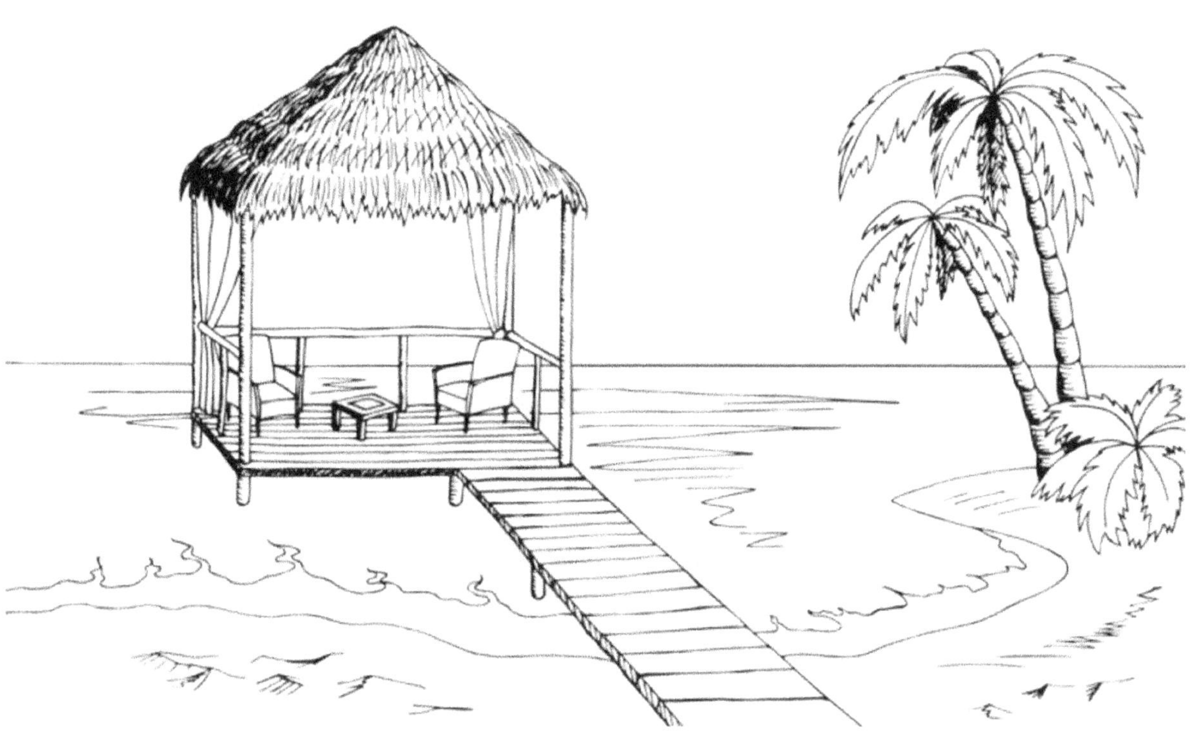

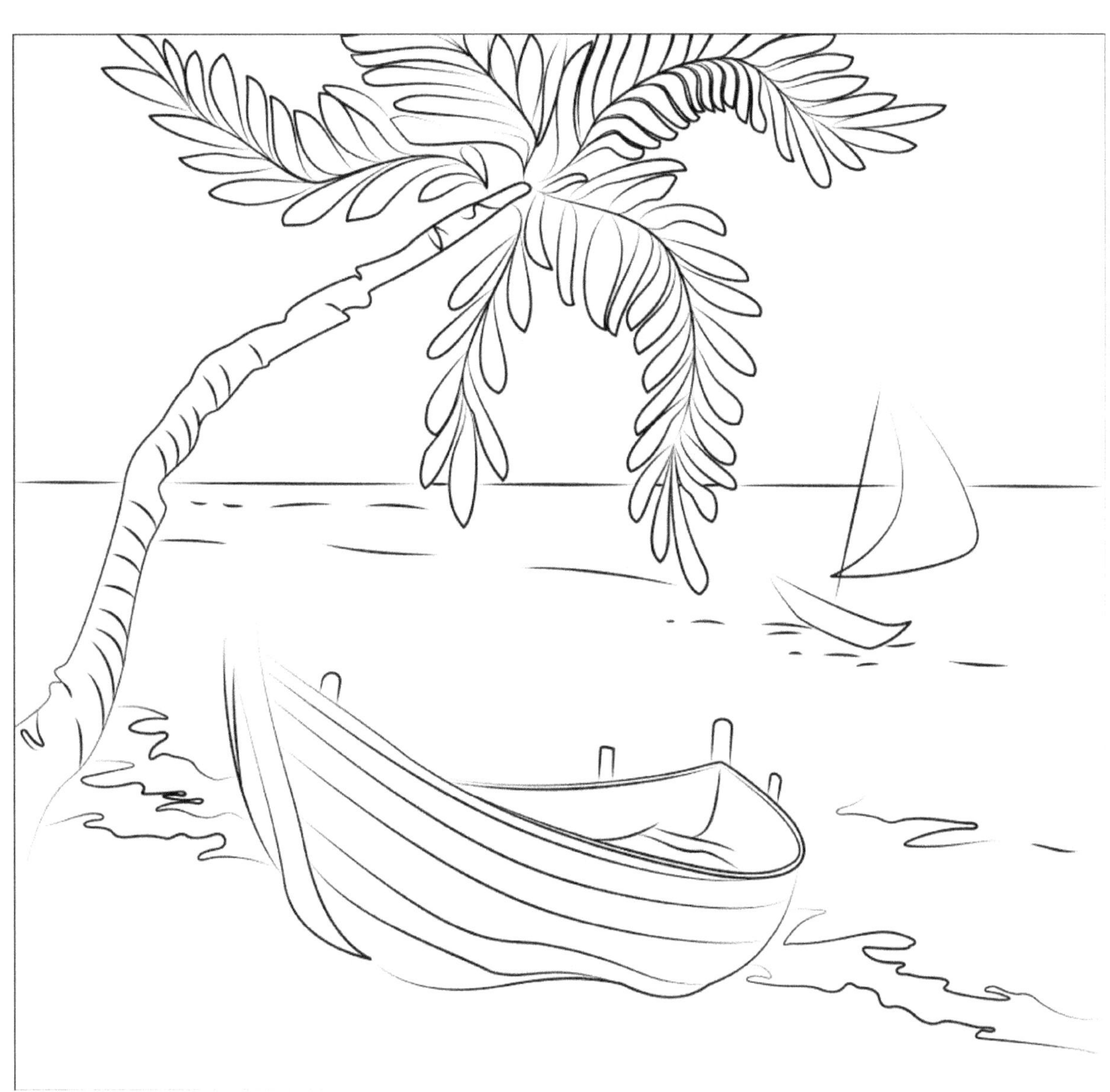

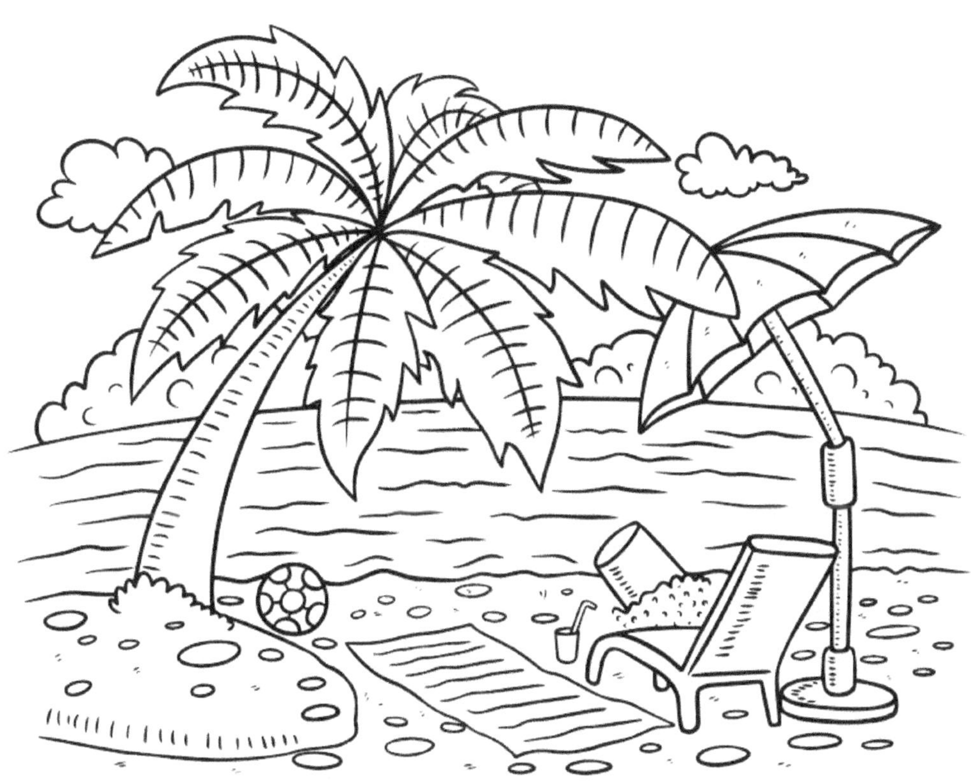

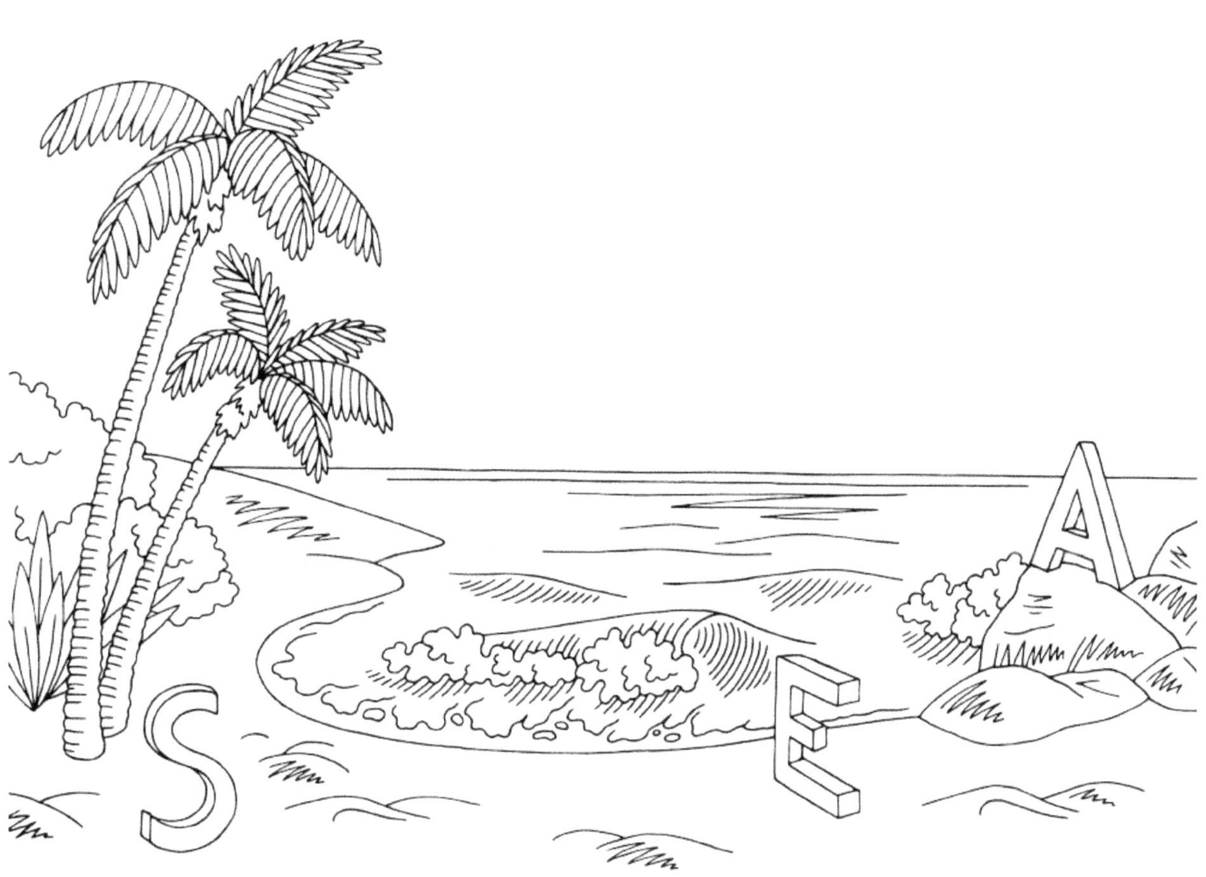

S
E
A

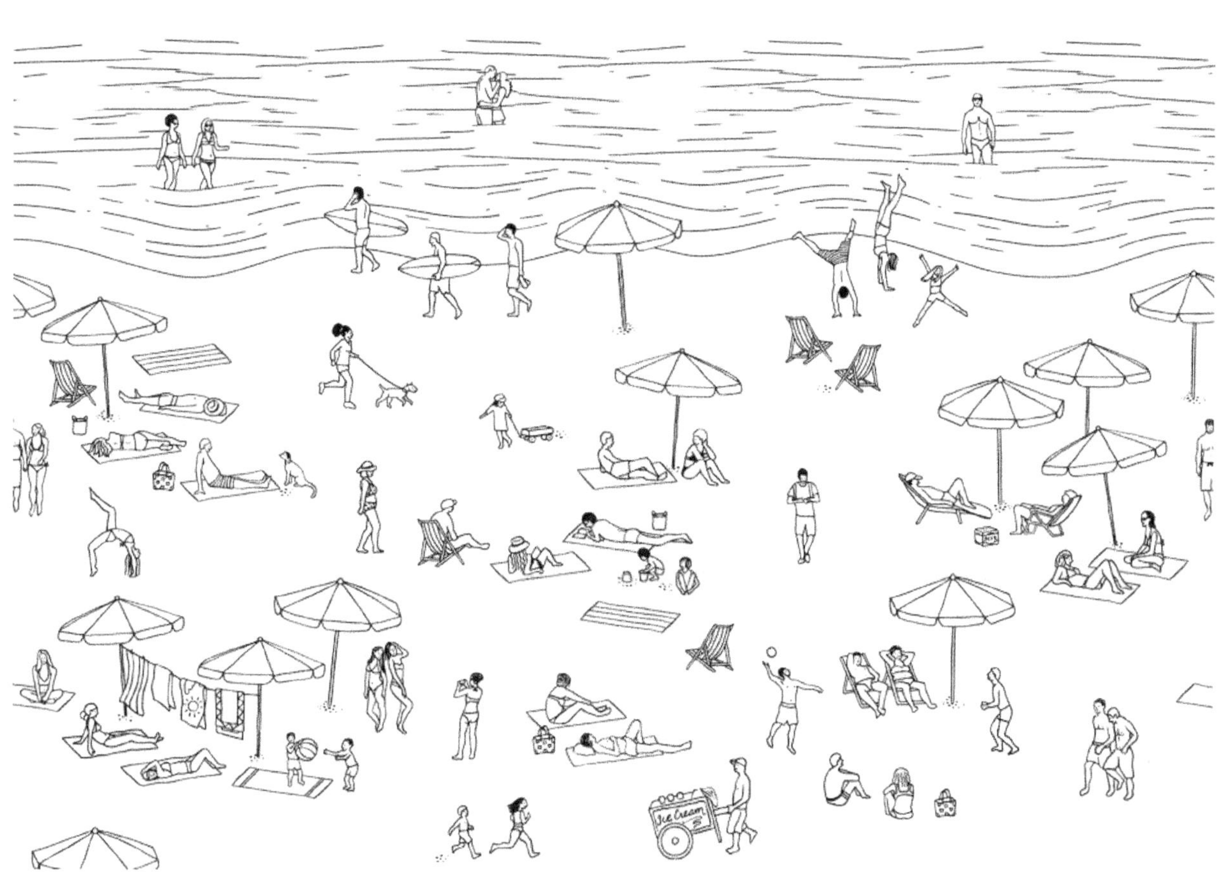
Ice Cream

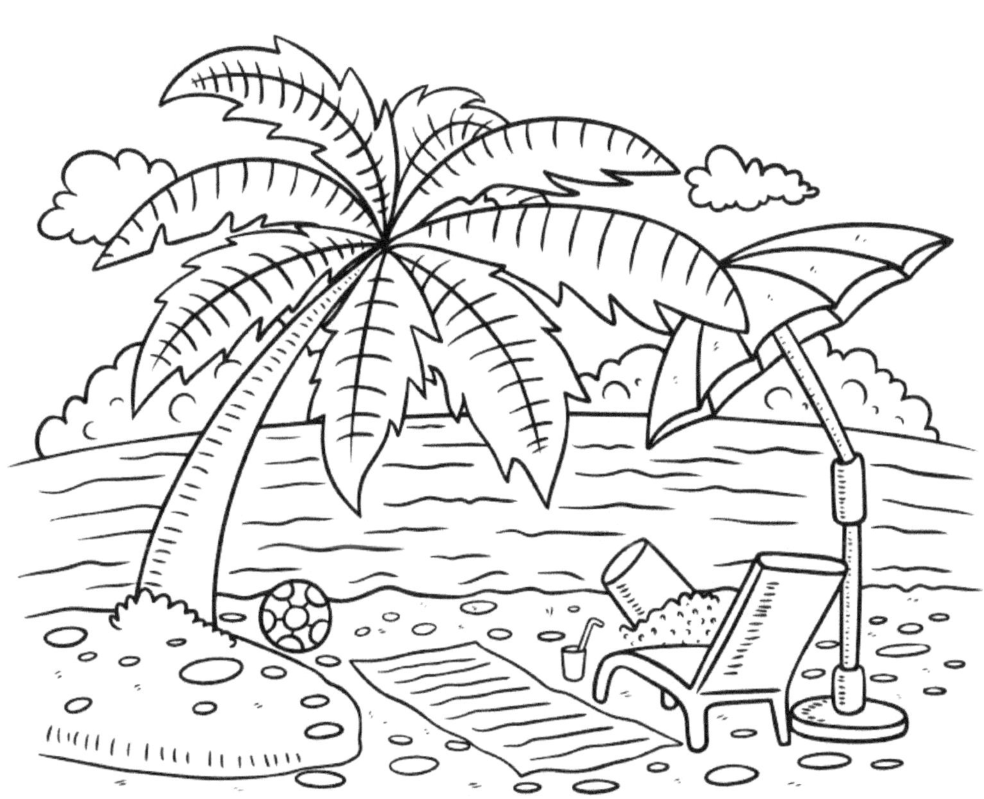

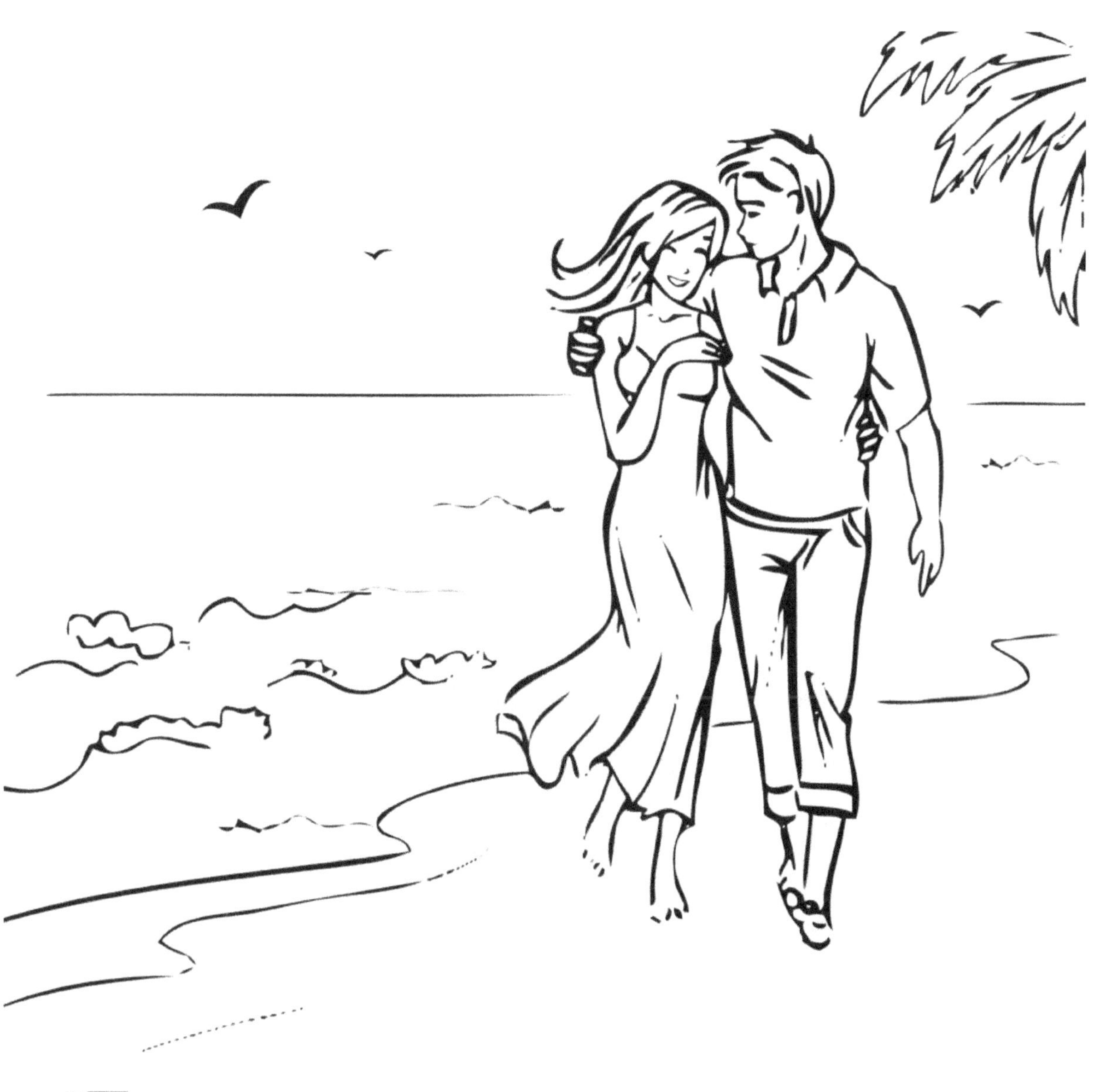

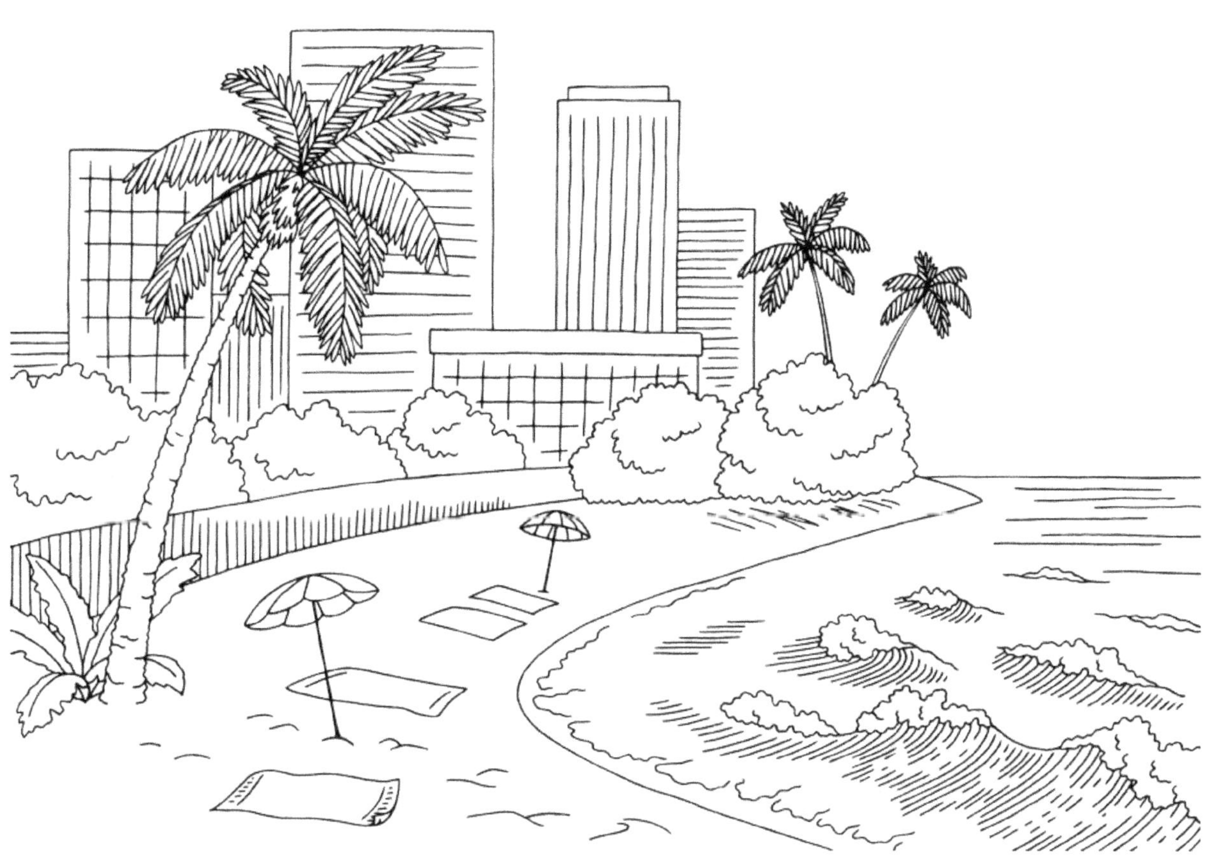

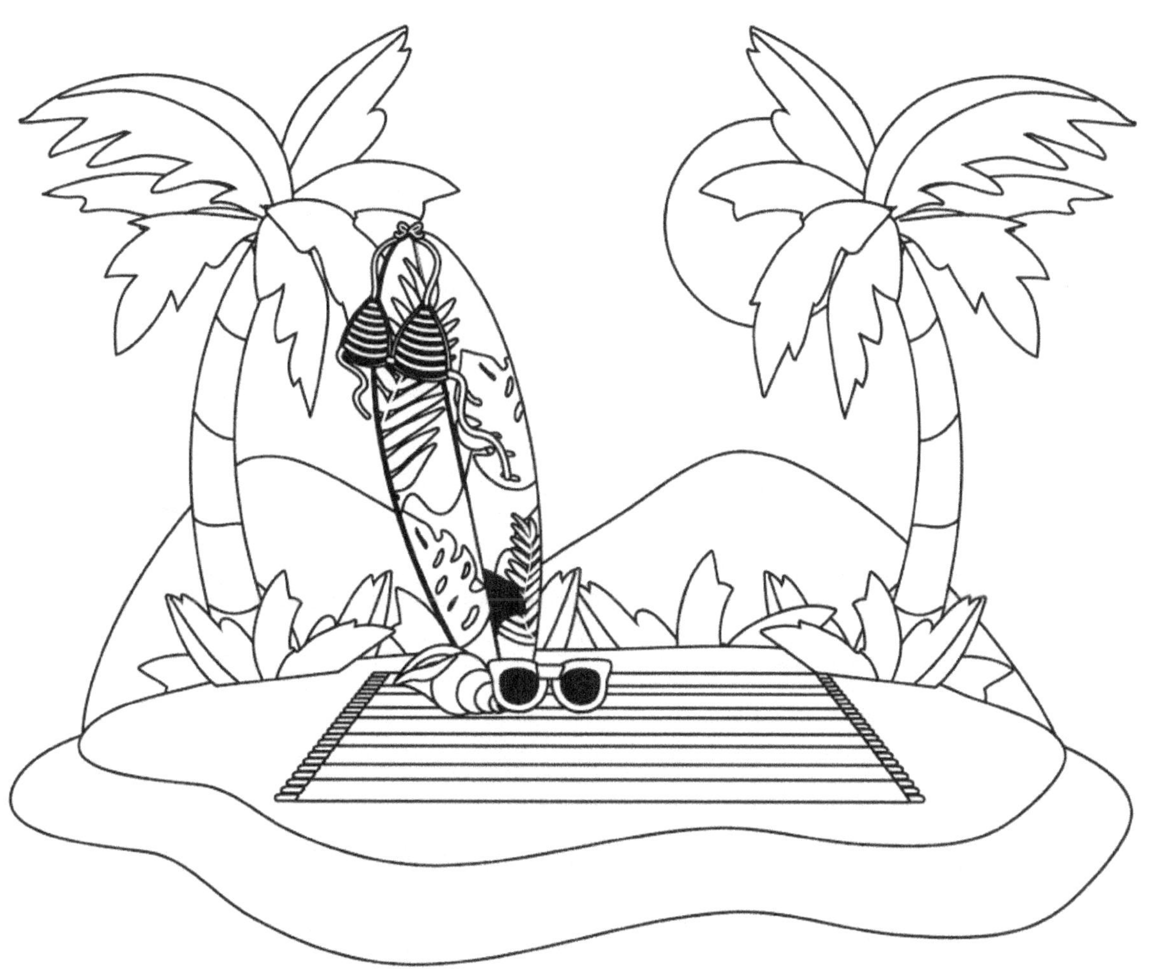

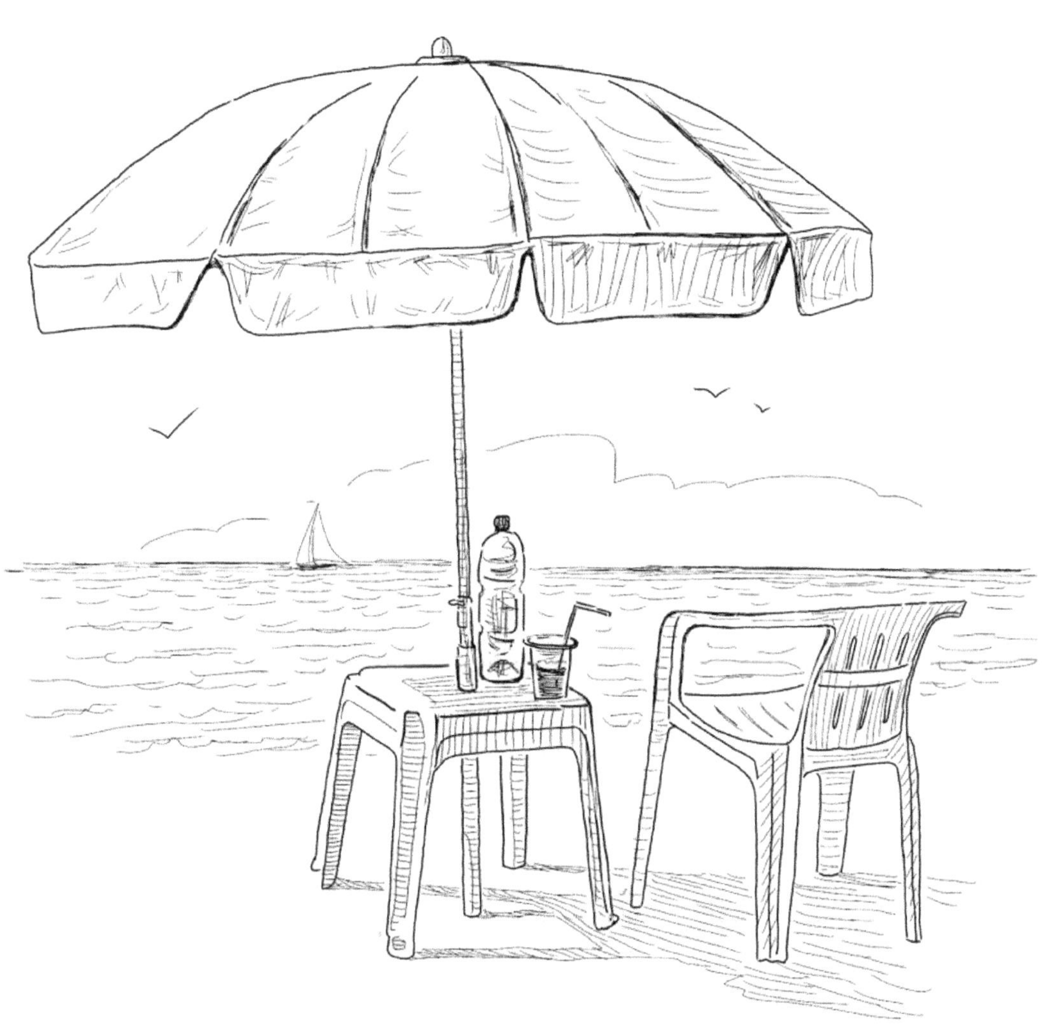

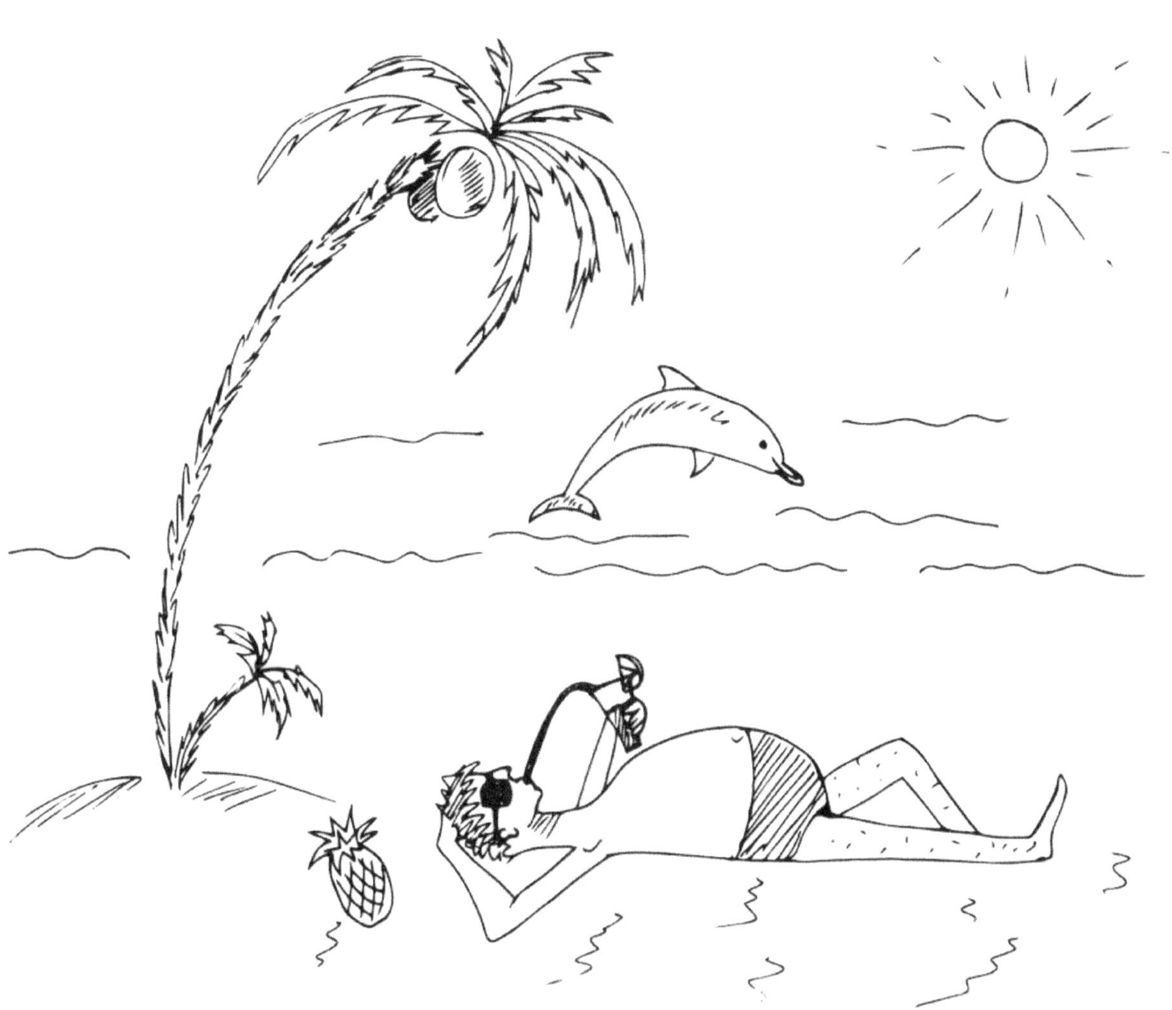

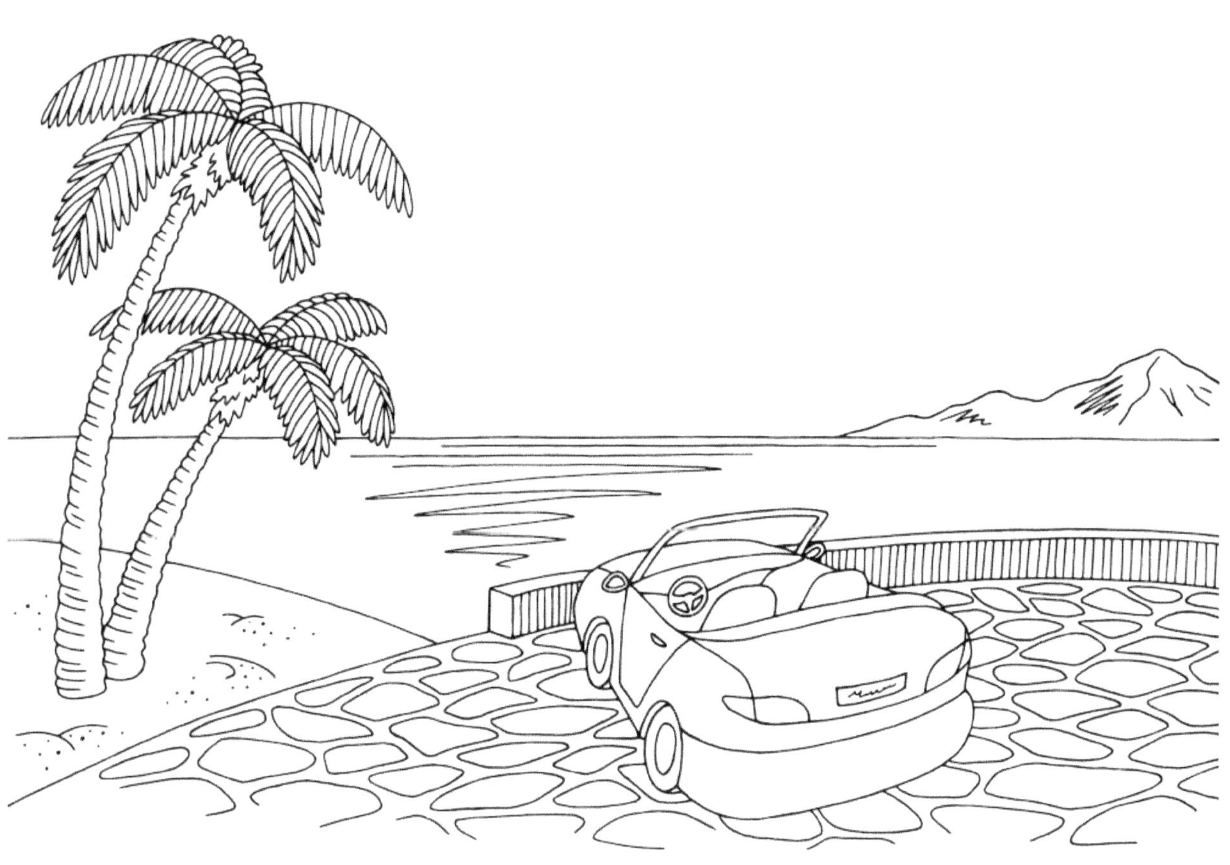

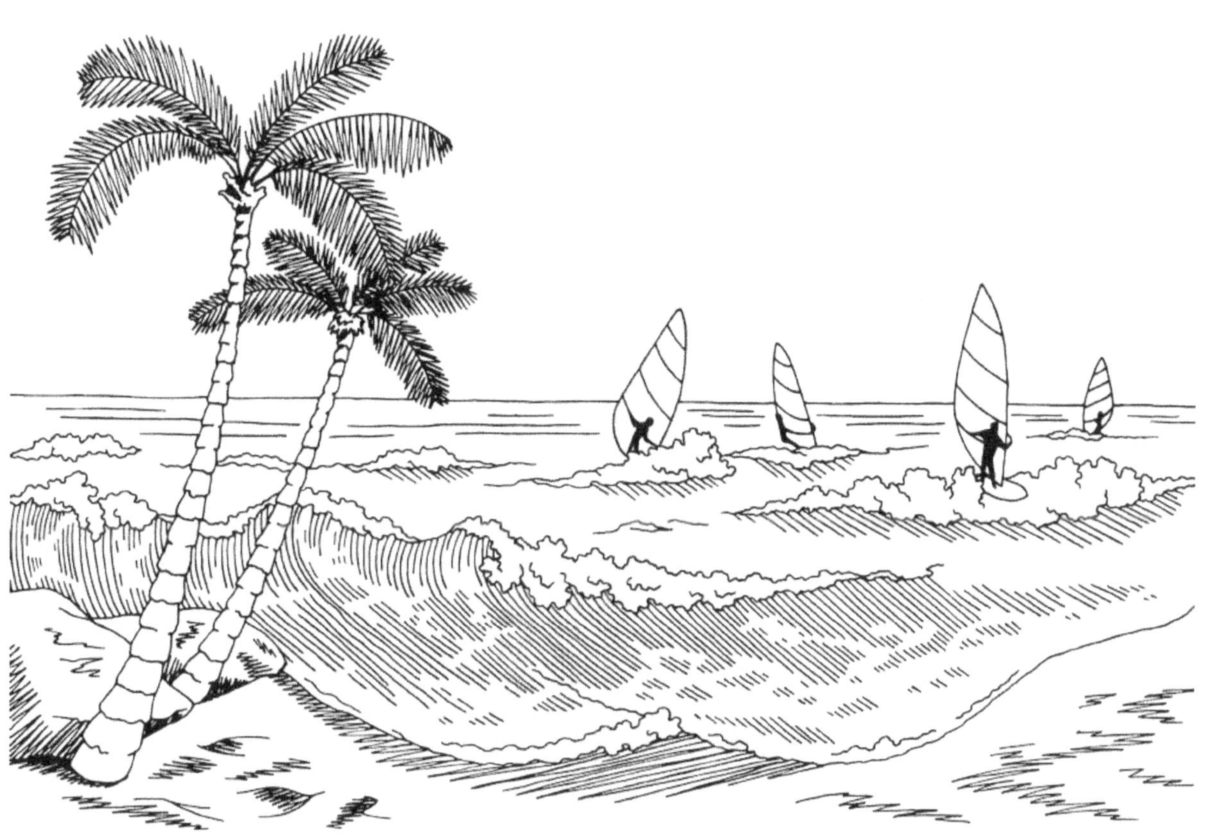

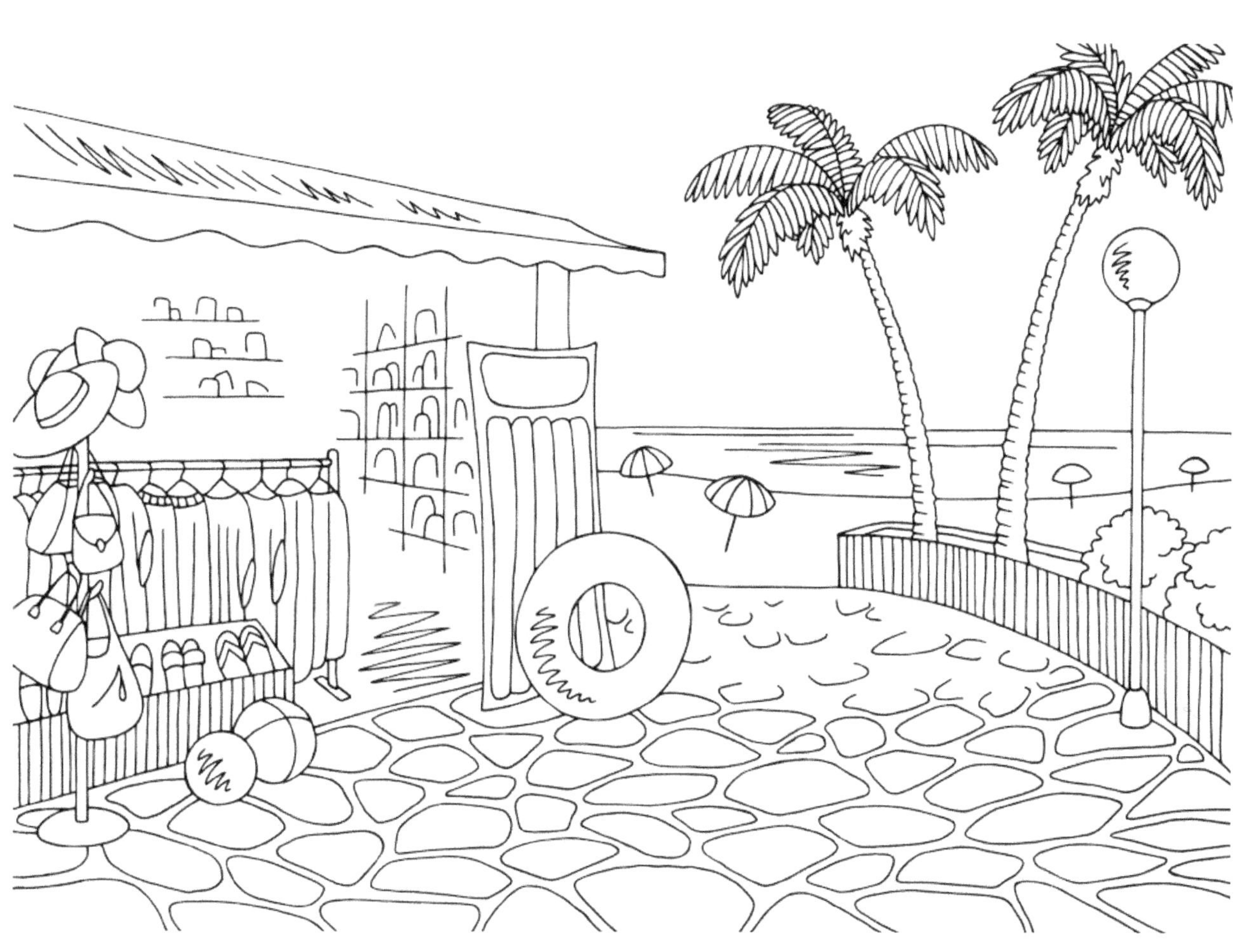

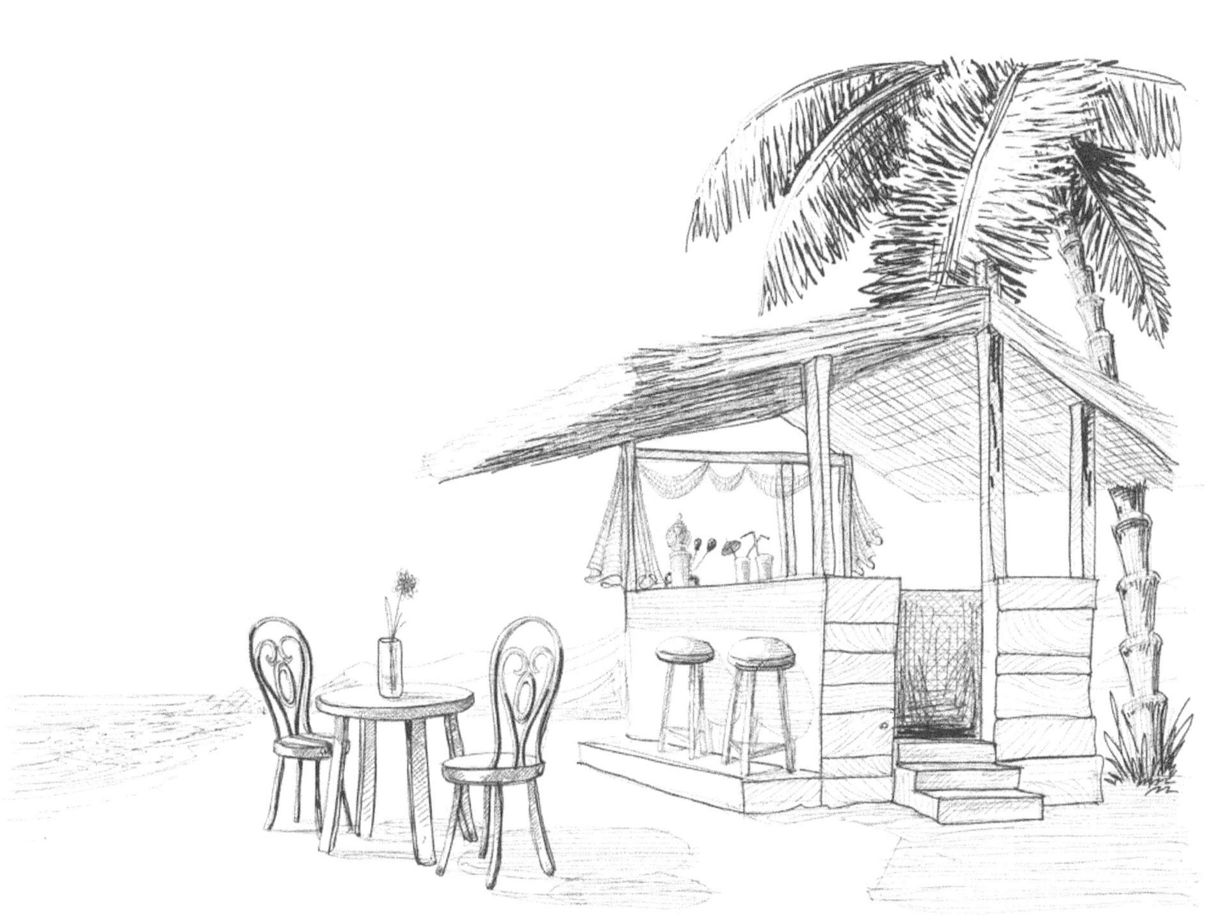

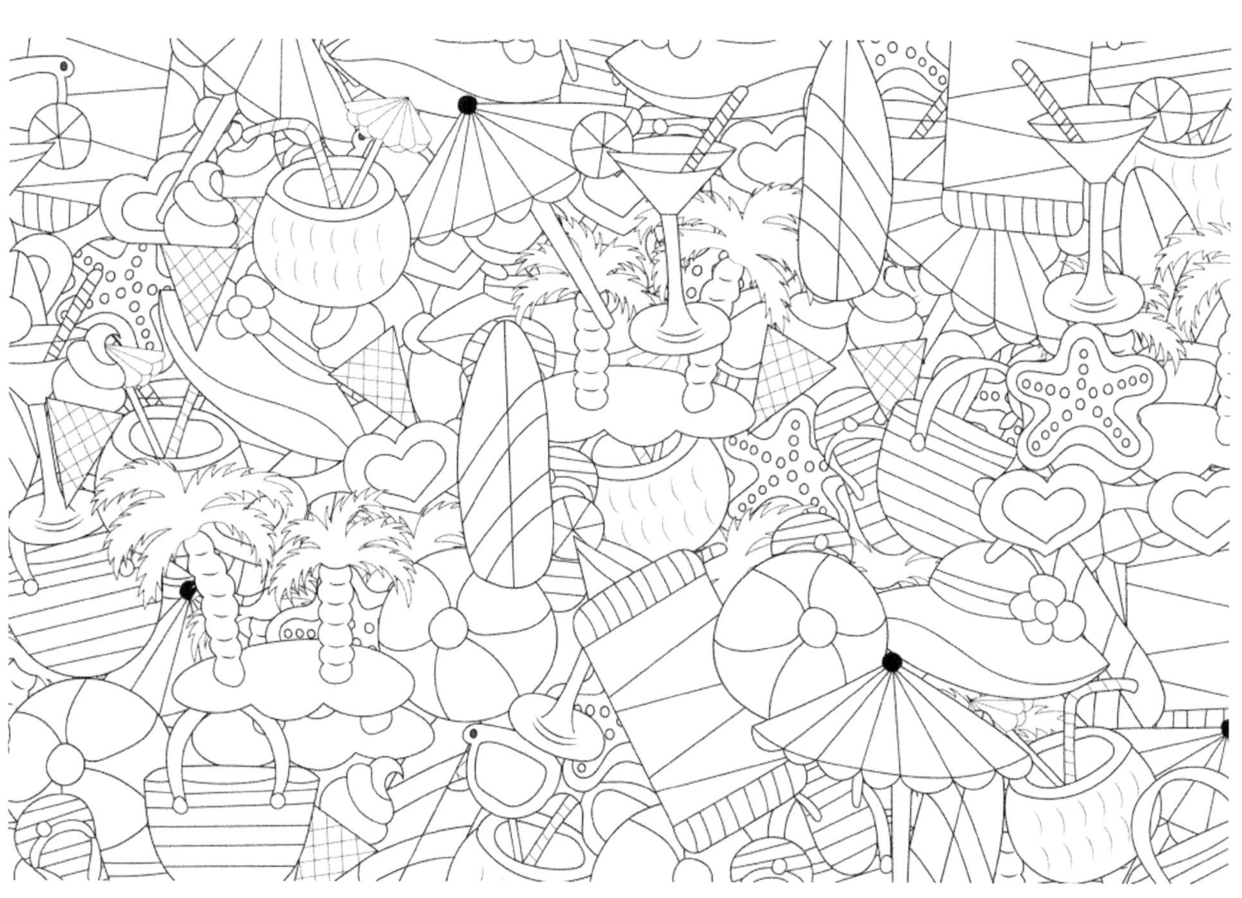

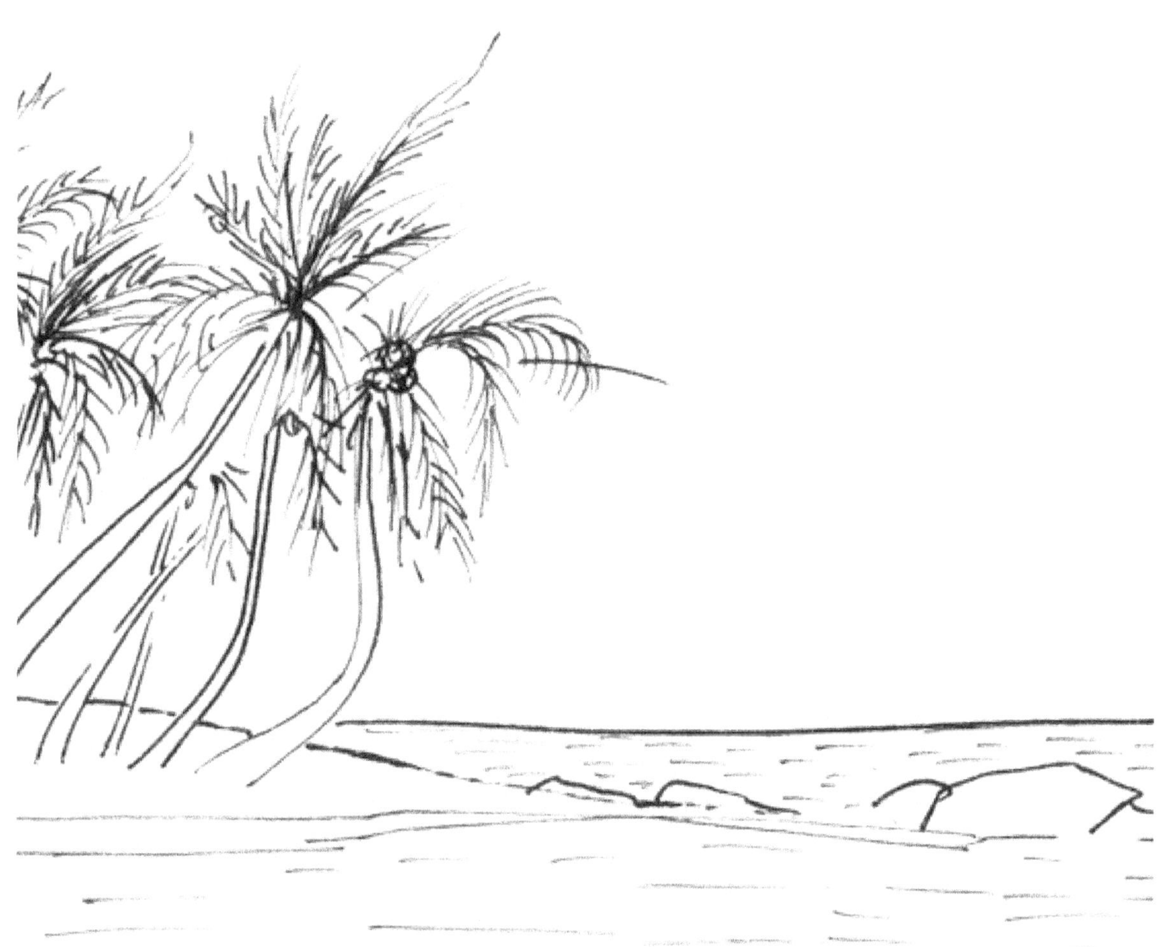

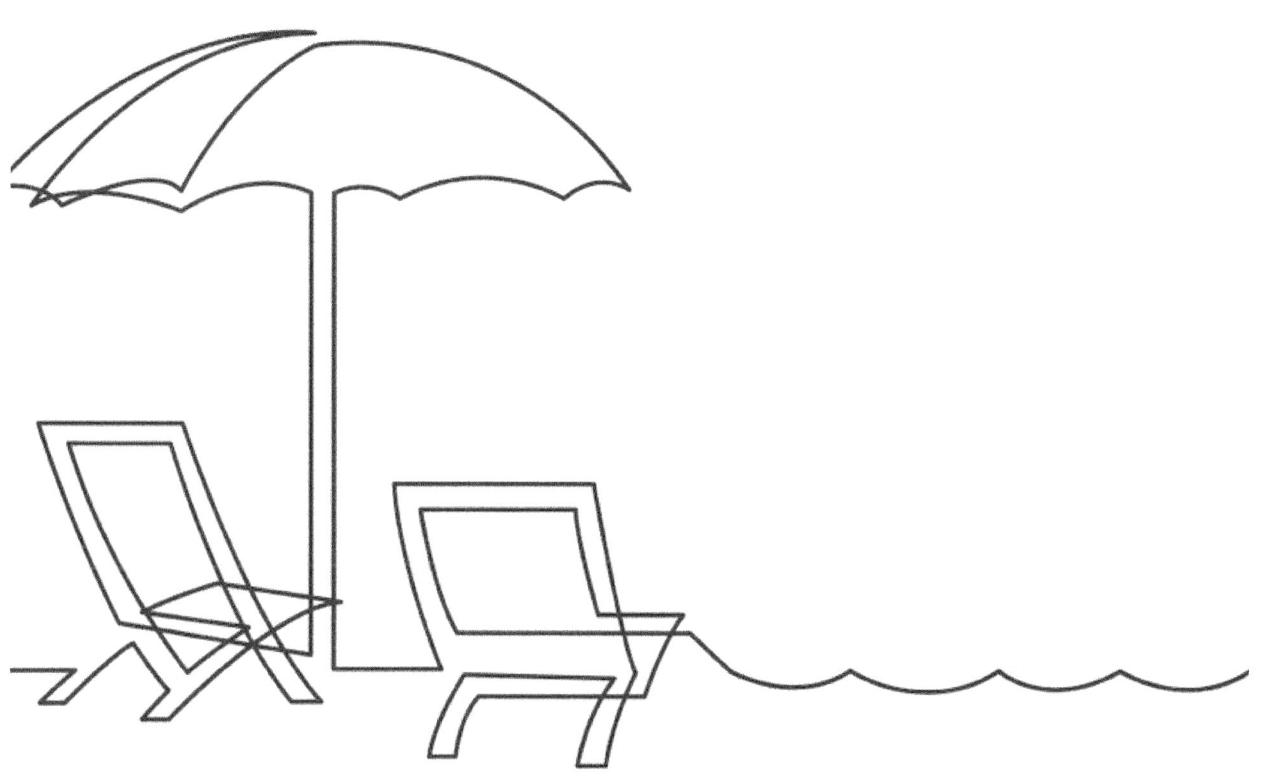

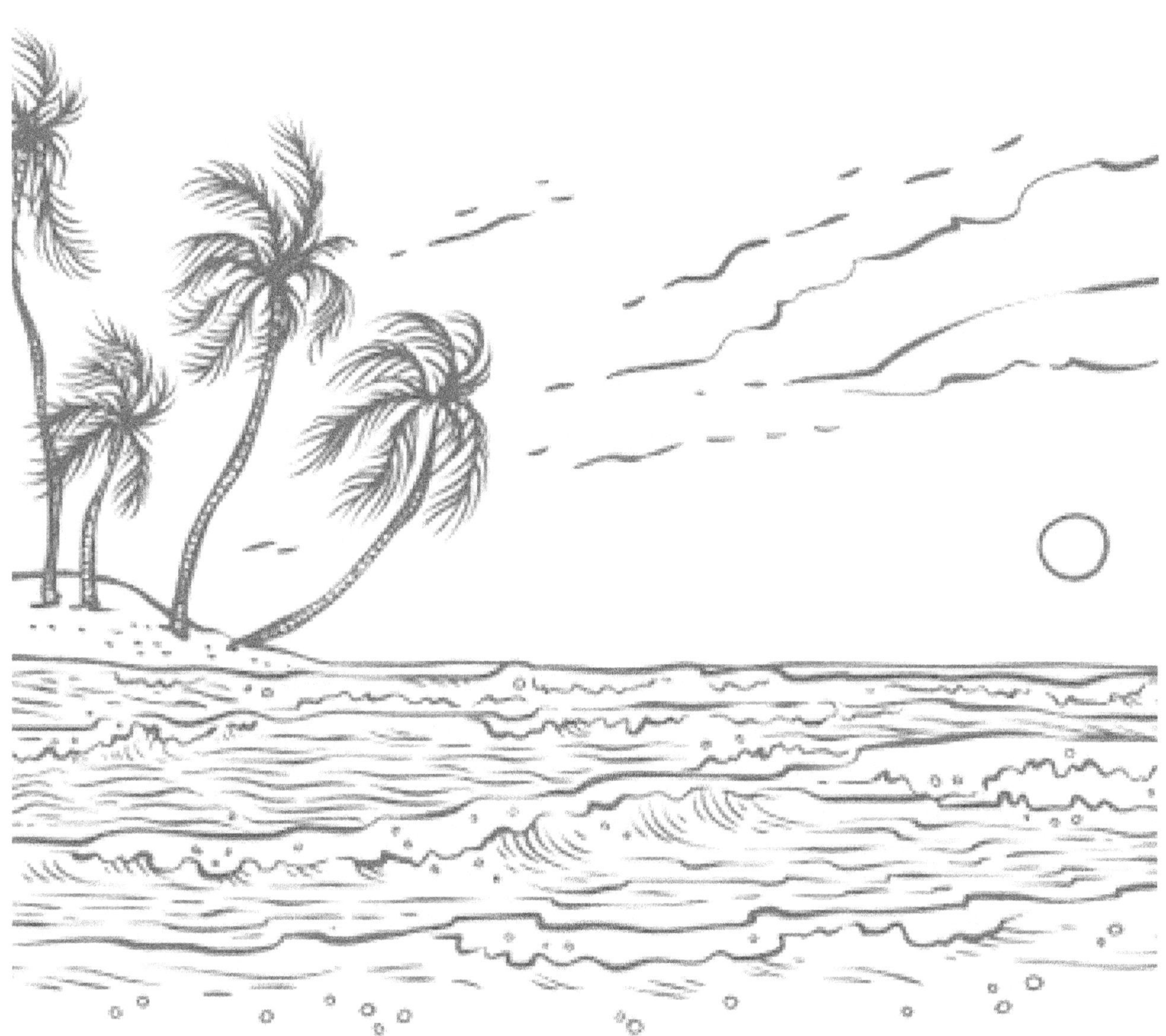

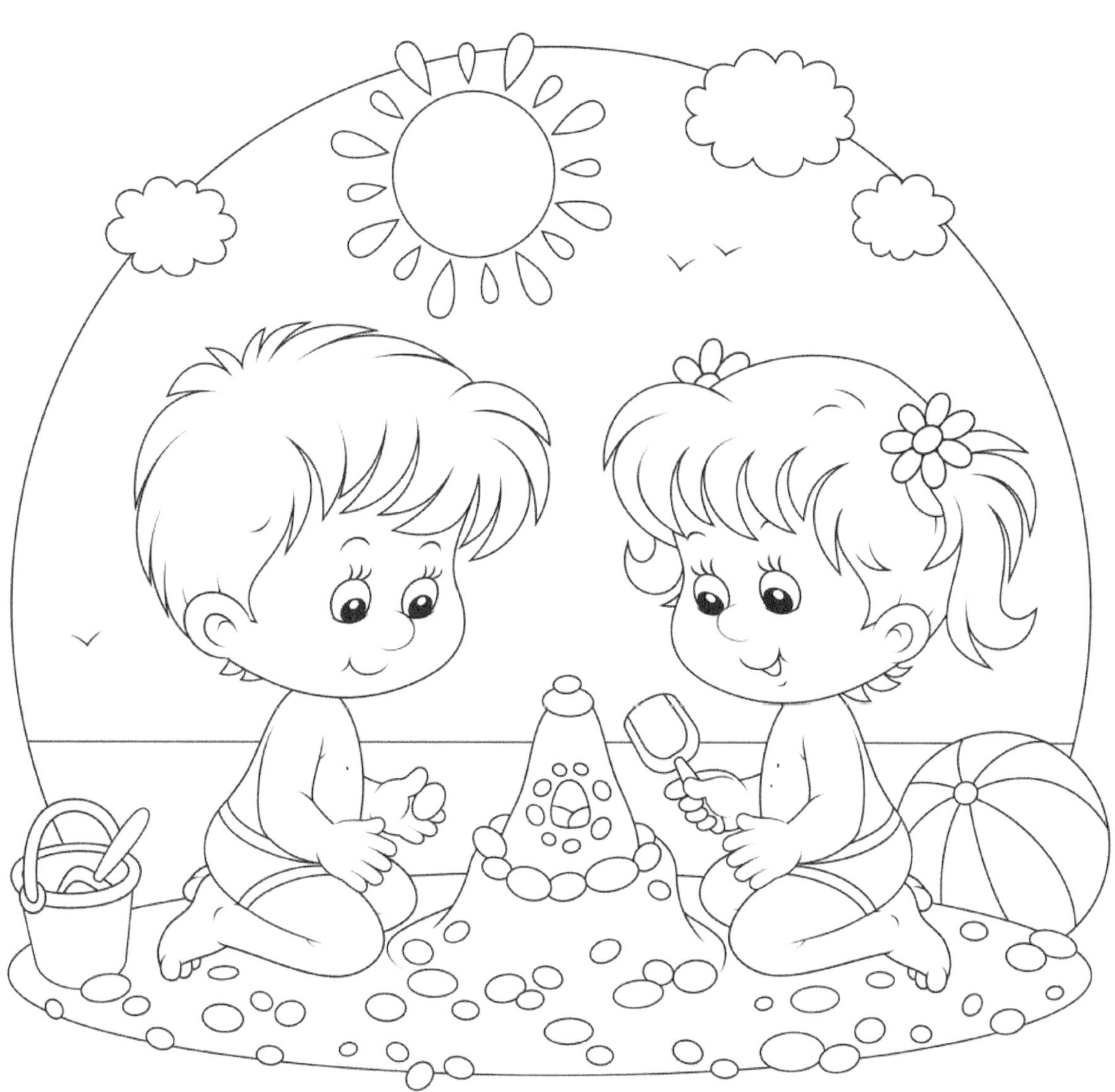

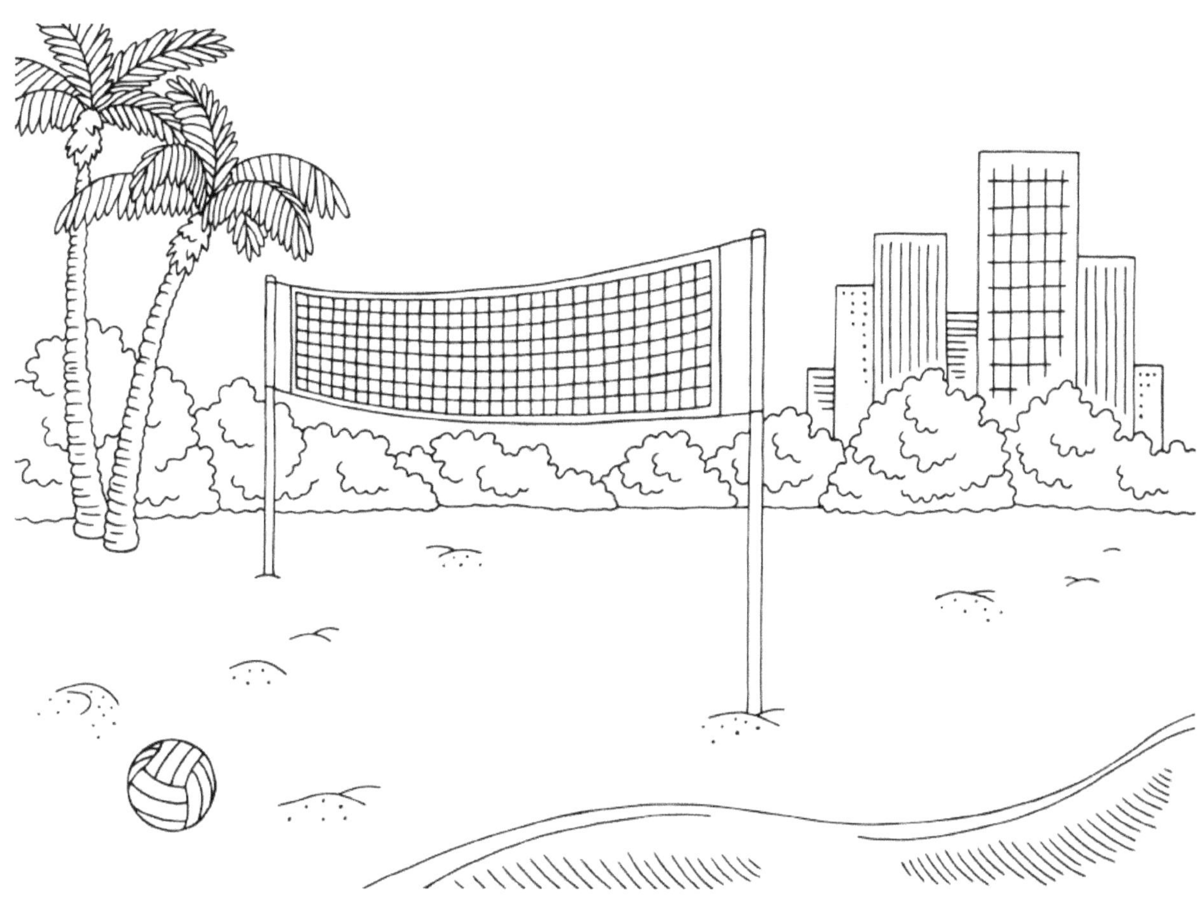

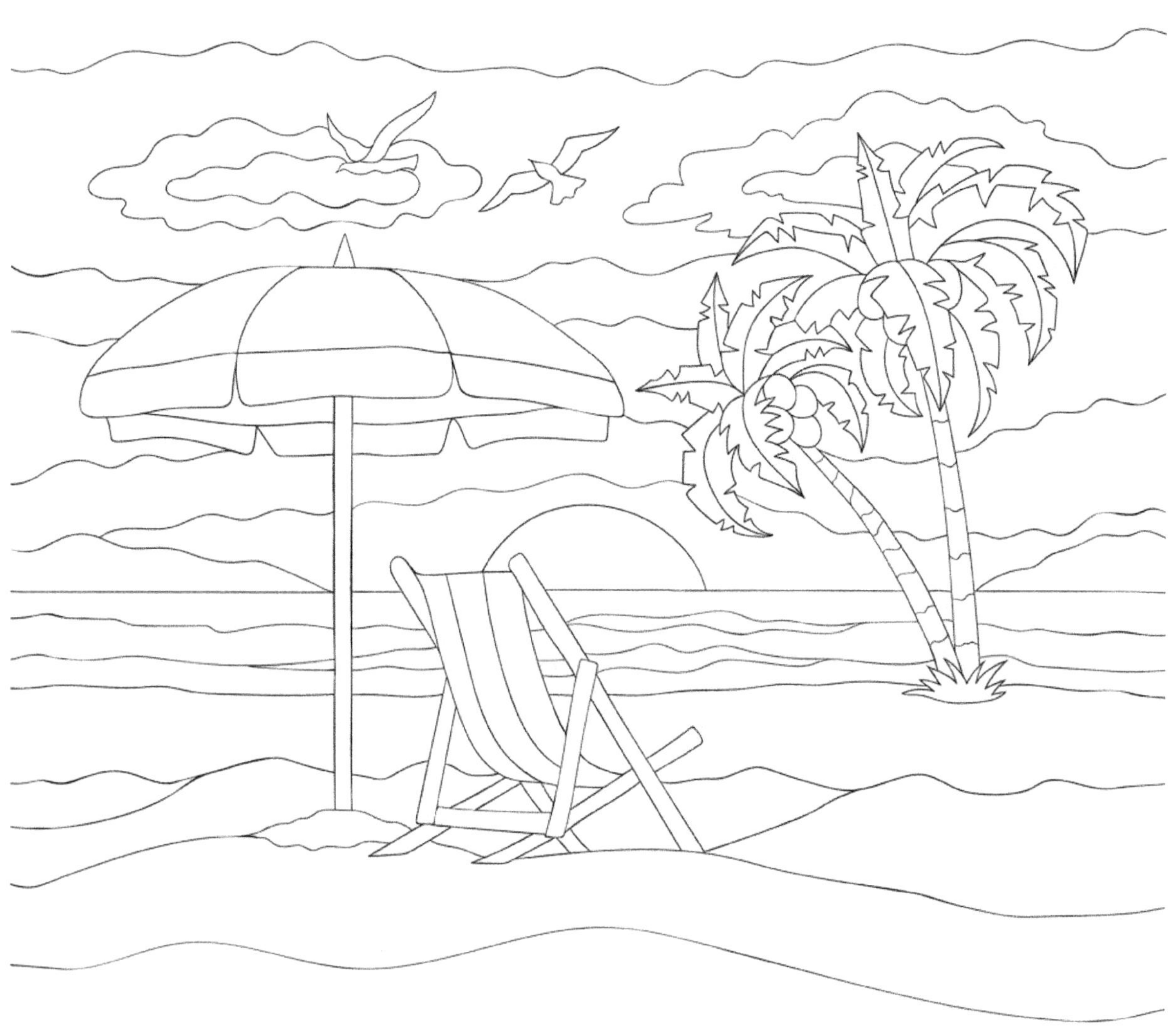

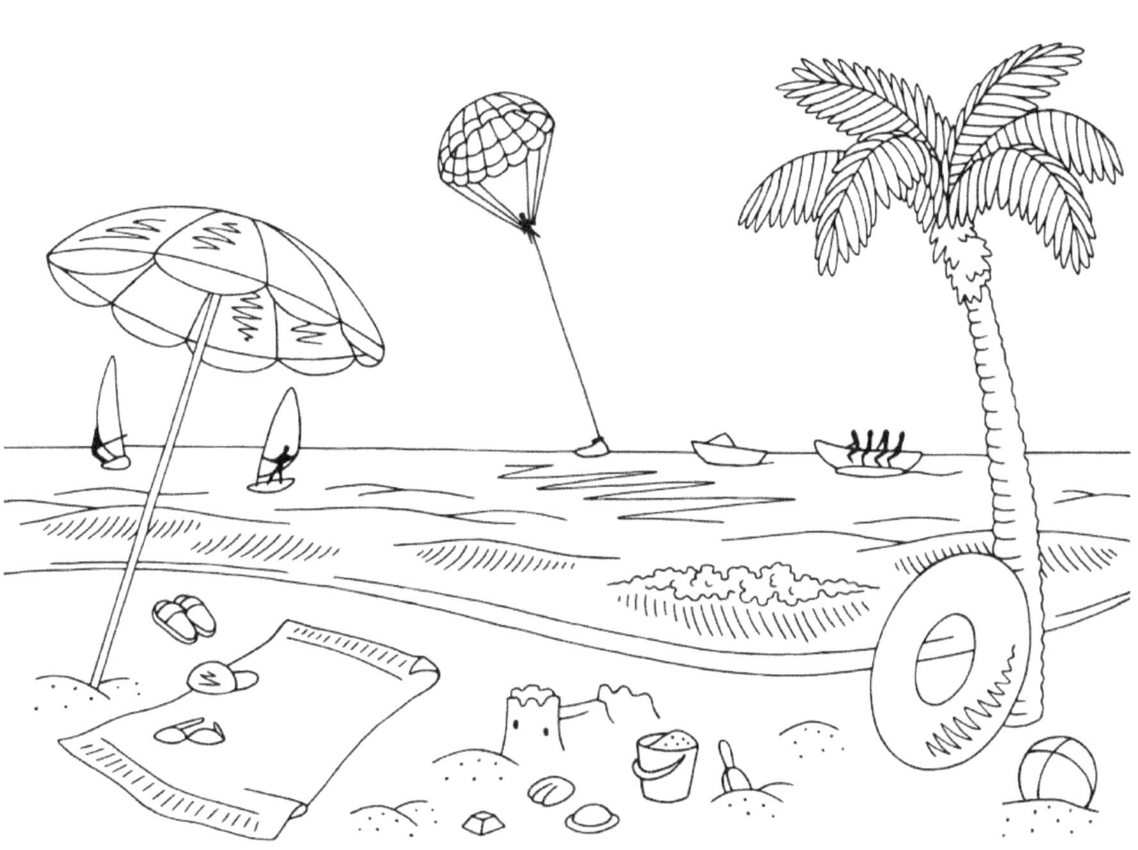

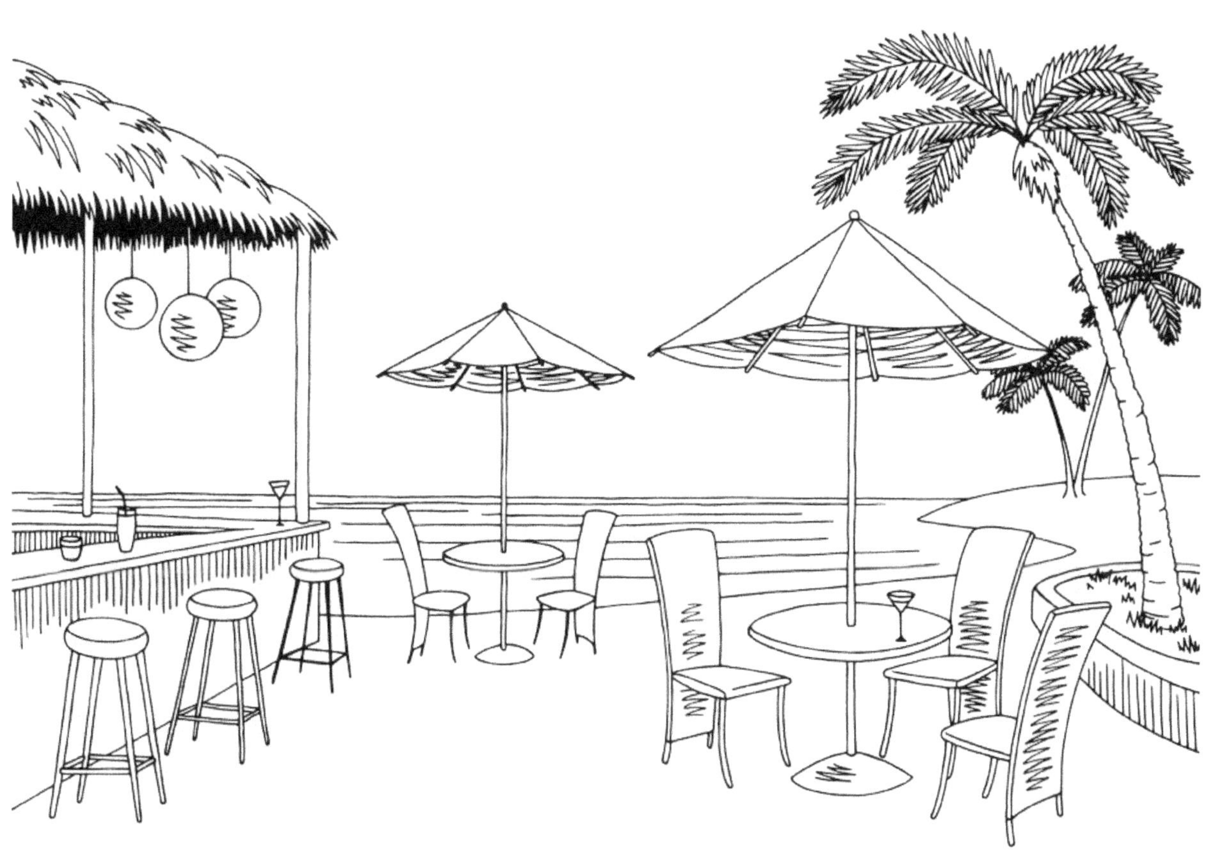

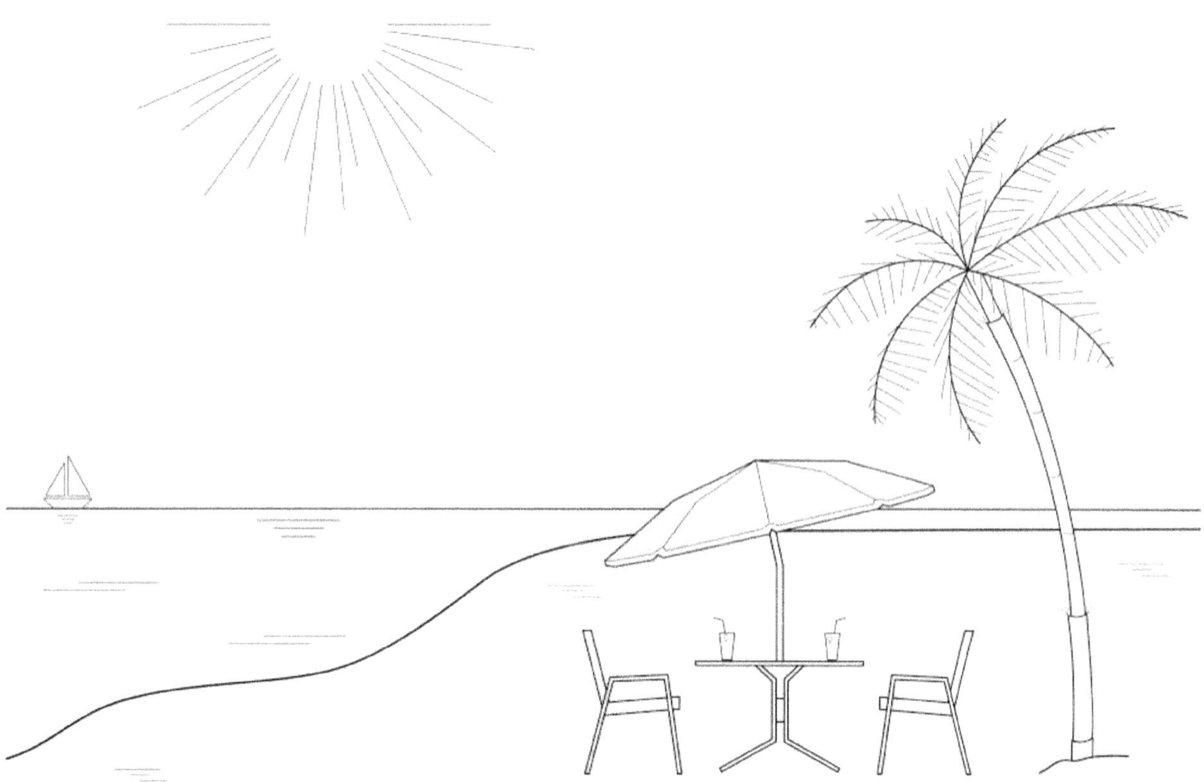

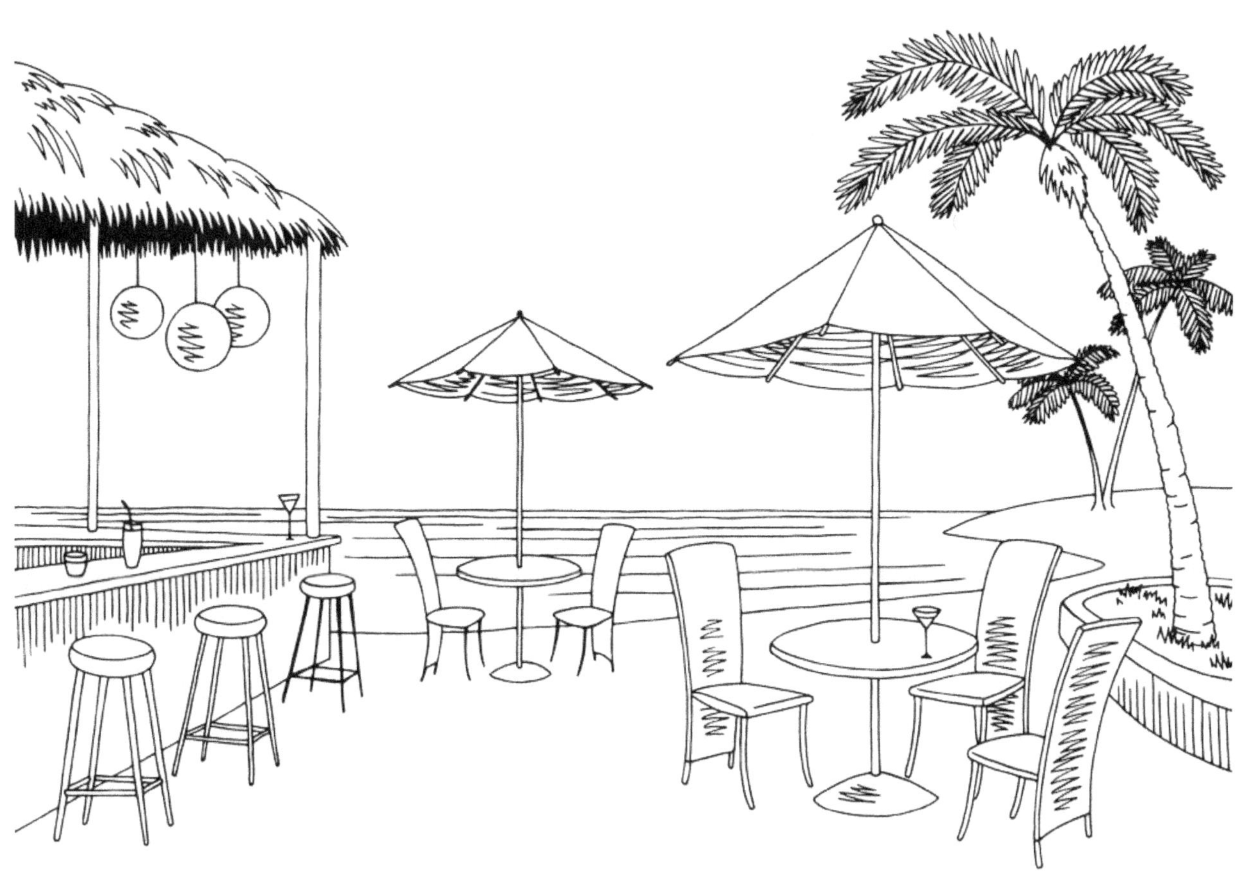